The Bird Whisperer
Volume Two

Dorothy Tilloson Kerr
and
Barbara Kerr Scott, Ph.D.

Prepared for Publication by
Barbara Kerr Scott

Biography

Volume Two is a continuation of *The Bird Whisperer*. I inherited several books of birding notes from my mother which she kept for nearly four decades. Volume two opens with several pages that were stapled together and tucked into the back of her first notebook. A formal preface is in volume one.

Born in 1921 and raised in Corpus Christi, Texas, Dorothy Tilloson's birth certificate notes "live birth" and indicates her name as Baby. She attended Corpus Christi public Schools, graduating from Corpus Christi High (now Miller) in 1939 and attended Del Mar College the following terms and again in the 1950's and 1962. She served as editor of her High School and Del Mar student newspapers (1938-1941). At Dailey's Camera Store where she worked, she met Robert (Bob) Kerr, a photographer. They were married Dec 7, 1941, while Pearl Harbor was being bombed, though they were unaware of that, of course.

A feature article about her in the Corpus Christi Times noted that "She has been a bird Watcher since high school days and in 1943 a woman in Dayton, Ohio got her interested in it seriously" (09/25/1953). This passion she shared with close family and friends throughout her life.

Two highlights I can remember from the fifties were when she met Roger Tory Peterson, whom I vaguely remember, and Lyndon Johnson's visit to the ornithology society meeting while he was a Texas Senator during the early efforts to save the Whooping Cranes. We visited the reserve at Austwell several times, but all I remember is sneaking around to try to sight the cranes. Her bird journals end just two months before she died.

For most of the last four years of her life she lived with her husband, Bob (Dad to me) in Zapata, Texas, often visiting the bird sanctuary several miles south along the Rio Grande, and at home cultivating the trust of many generations of Road Runners, Coo-Coo Birds she and Dad called them. Eventually these wild neighbors were hand fed and taught their fledglings to come up onto the porch for special hand delivered treats.

Dorothy Tilloson in a classroom at
Del Mar College, 1941

BIG BEND TRIP   (Round trip 2101 miles)

June ~~19~~ 20   Left C.C. 4:00 a.m. Sunday June ~~19~~ 20, 1954
                   clear, cool
hiway 9 to S.A.

nighthawks
mourning doves
pair scissortails
mockingbird
Cardinal
Crested flycatcher pair feeding young in nest in hollow limb
            (natural) of old limb about 12 feet from ground
            in new roadside park (still under construction)
            Hiway 9 about 10 mi. So. of Oakville
Mourning doves on hiway 1 or 2 every 100 feet or so (several
            dead) must be eating grain from trucks
& sparrows of some kind (Lark Sparrows, flash of white on tail)

Roadrunner
Boat-tailed grackles

San Antonio 8:00 a.m.
Zoo 8:30 to 10:30   Hot and Clear
            European Stork
          · White faced glossy Ibis
          · Spoonbill
          · Am. Flamingo
            Chilean Flamingo
          · Blue bill duck (swam under water--black head
                        wh. cheeks)
          · Wood duck
          · Mallard
          · Pintail
            Guinea hen
            Ostrich
            Emu
            Cassawary
          · Magpie
          · Crow
          · Great Horned owl
            hornbill
            Myna
          · Toucan
          · Oyster catcher
            Penguins (2 var.)
          · Turkey vultures
          · Black vultures
          · Caracara
          · Blue Jay

lunch at roadside park about 10 mi. outside S.A.

Indigo bunting
Buzzards
3 Deer

To --
Junction, Hot

Lark Sparrow
Mockingbird
Buzzard
little bird activity -- too hot

Junction 4:00 p.m. to--Sonora

Spotted Towee
pair Tanagers (Hepatica ?)

Sonora El. 2120   4:30 p.m.
Lots of birds but no time to stop

Ozona El. 2347 5 p.m.
Mocking birds sitting guard over rain puddles
Live Oak Creek
Swallows

Scissortail   Octillo
Mourning doves

Roadside Park west of Shieffeeld
Orchard Oriole   chased by tiny warbler (all yellow; tail rufous
underneath. At least on white wing bar. Yellow all around
eyes. Crown maybe darker.) Challenged oriole with insect-
like (not unpleasant, but dainty & musical) trill or buzz.
Also fem house finch.
Nighthawks

First day traveled 472 mi.

Monday 20- 21
Ft. Stockton   swam in Commanche springs
El. 2954

4 Ravens crossed road

out of Pecos   About 23 mi on hiway 285-- 84 Cliff Swallow
                    nests under low bridge over dry creek. Birds
                    swarming overhead while Bob made picture.
                    Jug-shapped made of many little pellets of
                    mud shapped like oversized vitamin capsules

Lunch on Black River, New Mexico (Jumping Cactus)

Black River Village   shortly after noon.   Made camp.
                    6:30 drove to Carlsbad caverns to hear
                    "bat lecture" by Ranger. Watched bats leave
                    cave. Est. by ranger to be 3/4 million
                    present now. -- Sounded like wind in cavern.
                    Could hear wing bones clicking -- like myrid s
                    of tiny insects.

Tuesday Morn. ~~21st~~ 22
Black River Village

          Ferruginous Pygmy owl chased bird from tree
          then landed on dead branch. Sat there about
          15 min. while we watched. (Looked like part
          of branch) then flew

<u>Carlsbad Caverns</u>
          Crested flycatchers carrying insects into
          mouth of cave

Indigo buntings
House finch, male
 Bullock's Orioles, male & fem
 Western kingbird (yellow belly)
 Summer tanager

 Scaled Q uail sitting on fence
 Pyrrhuloxia, male singing in tree top. (reminescent of
                cardinal, more repitous I think
 Last night--cottonwood tree limb cracked & broke about 50
                feet from by bed.

 Centipede & tranatulas crossing the road, many of them.

<u>At the Caverns</u>

 After going thru (walked down and ~~upt~~, both --lunch in caverns)
 ~~xxxkk~~ walked Nature trail -- walked down to old bat cave shaft

 Desert Sparrow

<u>Guadalupe Pass</u>
 El. 5288
 At foot of El Capitan, many red-barked madrona trees

<u>Just before Van Horne</u>

 Swainson's Hawk (normal phase)

       23
 Wed. ~~22~~nd
 Roadside park Hiway 290
 Dessert Sparrows

 5 mi. from Ft. Davis

 214 swallow nests under bridge

 McDonald Obwervatory 1:30 p.m.
 Lecture ture: 3rd largest tele. in world; Mt. Locke el. 6791;
                highest point om St. Hiway. Mountains can be
                seen 100 mi. away in Mexico

Wed. 22nd. night and Thrusday 23rd
<u>The Basin</u>

Deer in camp early morning
Pair House finches   feeding young in top of maquey plant
Couch's jays, Brown headed cowbirds, squirrels feeding at camp
                                        side on bird seed, cracked pecans,
                                        and bread crums.

hiked <u>Window Trail</u>   Got lost coming back; gone 3½ hours;
                                        Must have walked lo mi.

Black-chinned hummers,
Scott's orioles
Couch's Jays

<u>Langtry</u>   Judge Roy Bean's Office

Spent night in roadside park on Pecos

~~Thursday~~
Friday
Pecos River Canyon

Cardinals   Can see where Pecos flows into Rio Grande
Tanager   Coon came into camp; eating Scraps thrown over
                 brideg

<u>Walk Lake</u>

Orchard Oriole
Titmice
Red-eyed Cowbird
Scissortails again--none seen from N. Mex. to here
Mockers   becoming plentiful again

<u>Devil's Lake</u>
arrived just before noon

Out in Boat:
White wing dove sitting on willow limb out over water in little
                 slough
Mourning dove on nest same site
Boat tail Grackles
Orchard orioles
Bewick's Wren

Canyon Wren--singing high above us at top of sheer canyon wall
                 studded with cactus, agave and desert shrubs.
                 song beautiful, bell-like, whistle ending in
                 trill.
                 Went into cave on canyon wall Nothing there
                 except remains of fires evidently built by
                 fishermen in winter to keep warm
                 collected rock plants and cactus while ~~baby~~
                 Bob and kids fished.

Friday Cont.

Still in boat:
Red wings -- pair every 50 feet or so in cattails and reeds
                bordering lake
Green Heron   flushed and flew across the lake--outstanding
                in the early evening light. Wings looked blue
                feet bright red.

Dusk:
Goatsucker of some kind drinking from lake on the wing like
                swallows.
2 goatsuckers flew over calling to each other--gutteral call
                ending in buzz similiar to nighthawk. White
                wing patches.

Saturday Devil's lake (camped down by water)

Started raining before dawn, all day Sat. and Sat. night.
we moved to top of a hill. Camp area completely covered.
Car and tents left down there completely under water. Radio
says 5.97 " at C.P.L. plant about 1 mil away

Sunday 27th
Rained light all day; tried to dry out clothes but not very
successful. Finally decided to try to get out. Made it to
hiway about 5 p.m. after fording 3 "wet weather crossings"
and skidding on several clay hills. Glad we didn't try
it earlier this morning. One of them had 17feet of water
going over.

Cloud burst at Ozona sent many more tons of water into Devils
river after we left. Bridge where we spent Thurs. night
on Pecos went out. Worst flood in History of Rio Grande.
(see Newspaper clippings)

Sunday night
Garner state park
Skunk nosing around camp.
started raining here Mon. morn. so we left.
decided to go on to Eagle pass and Falcon Dam to watch flood

MONDAY

Carrizo Springs

2 mockers chasing Raven (white necked)
large dove (long tail) sitting on wire in pasture
Orchard Oriole
mockers, scissor tails, mourning doves, buzzards, unid. sparrows,
6 to 10 vultures sitting on tree; unid. hawk flew right in
front of car
Dedided to go to Laredo to follow flood, Accord. to radio,
biggest flood in history of Rio Grande. More rain on Devil's
River. 500 people stranded at Langtry on train and auto. 14
Helicopters flying them out. These were the ones we say while
leaving River Road just be fore Del Rio

TEXAS ORNITHOLOGICAL SOCIETY

DEDICATED TO THE OBSERVATION, STUDY
AND CONSERVATION OF BIRDS IN TEXAS

NEWSLETTER	VOLUME VI	NUMBER 11	December 10, 1958

* * * * * * * * * * * *

OFFICERS OF THE TEXAS ORNITHOLOGICAL SOCIETY

President: A. Earl Jourde, 1017 Stirman St., Corpus Christi
Vice-President: Carrie Holcomb, 1008 Missouri, Houston 6
Secretary-Treasurer: Mrs. Mike O'Neil, 1311 Bonham, Commerce
Corresponding Secretary: Mrs. Robert B. Kerr, 1337 Maryland, Corpus Christi
Editor: Mrs. J. W. LeSassier, 1611 W. Indiana, Midland

Official Bird: Scissor-tailed Flycatcher

We returned a number of times during 1957. To my list I added Long-billed Curlews, Laughing Gulls, Least and Common Terns, Brown-headed Cowbirds, Cliff Swallows, Willets, Nighthawks, Ruddy Turnstones, and Black-necked Stilts. On August 27, I noted "about 75 Spoonbills (adult and immature) feeding and 25 Wood Ibis feeding and resting in the marshes at 2:30 PM -- countless birds in the rookery -- stopped about 1000 feet from the rookery -- hundreds of birds in marsh to left of road (over 200 in one compact group; others scattered over a square mile or so in various-size groups). Snowy and Common Egrets, Tricolored Herons, Spoonbills, Wood Ibis and Grackles -- all scrambled up together -- hundreds more in the rookery and in the edge of the water. Over 100 White Pelicans off to the west away from the other birds".

It was on this trip that we met Dr. Bauer, President of the Copano Sportsmen's Club, and learned of his interest in the heronry. He had come to check on the young in the nests, and told us of his concern about parties camping among the nests. This was then a bad situation. Many times we saw campers park under trees containing birds and begin to unload fishing, cooking, and sleeping gear, seemingly unconcerned by the birds' screaming overhead or the youngs' tumbling through the branches trying to hide.

It was also on this trip that I recorded the following: "7:20 PM. Birds by the hundreds, flowing into the marshes and the rookery -- the trees are white with them, like so many blossoms -- flock after flock arriving from all directions, except from the east over Copano Bay ..... 7:30 PM. Almost dark and still the birds come -- the sky is filled with them as far as you can see. Snowy Egrets and Tricolored Herons coming in low; Pelicans and Great Blue Herons coming in high and dropping abruptly. Heard them well, after it was too dark to see".

I have seen only one scavenger, other than the pack rats and kangaroo mice, at the site -- a Turkey Vulture was immediately chased off by a Black Skimmer, who flew just above him, diving at his back. I watched until they were tiny specks in the distance. A short time later the Black Skimmer returned alone.

We can only hope for good weather during the next spring and summer so that some of us can get some accurate counts of the nesting birds.

POSTCRIPT from Dr. Bauer: "I brought this matter (the heronry) up before the Game and Fish Commission, but as of October 14, have heard nothing from them ... This land is under lease and belongs to the State. The lease has one more year to go. I am interested in getting a special act through the Legislature to get a permanent lease on this land ... and hand it over to the Audubon Society so that proper signs can be put up and a Game Warden be put in charge during the nesting season. Campers kill small birds and use them for Crab bait; they also camp near the nesting ground which disturbs the birds."

* * * * * * * * * * * *

OFFICERS OF THE TEXAS ORNITHOLOGICAL SOCIETY

President: A. Earl Jourde, 1017 Stirman St., Corpus Christi
Vice-President: Carrie Holcomb, 1008 Missouri, Houston 6
Secretary-Treasurer: Mrs. Mike O'Neil, 1311 Bonham, Commerce
Corresponding Secretary: Mrs. Robert B. Kerr, 1337 Maryland, Corpus Christi
Editor: Mrs. J. W. LeSassier, 1611 W. Indiana, Midland

Official Bird: Scissor-tailed Flycatcher

The work of being a good regional director is time-consuming, requires iniative and energy, and is easily discouraged if members do not respond. On the other hand, it has been suggested that perhaps some directors are inactive only because they do not understand their duties and responsibilities. A review of the original purposes of the regions and directors would indicate that the follow- ing statement might summarize the proper functions of a regional director:

1. Promote regional activities (field trips, meetings, conservation,
    education, publicity).
2. Assist TOS officers in the conducting of the TOS program and in
    promoting TOS objectives.
3. Advise and counsel TOS officers concerning:
    a. Local and regional needs wherein the state organization can
        be useful.
    b. Statewide and nationwide needs which should be included in
        the TOS program.

Formation of the new Committee on Constitution and By-laws is underway. Meanwhile, the chairman requests that all members of TOS consider the problem which was presented to the Executive Board concerning regions and directors, and that any member who is willing to express his opinion and who desires to participate in TOS affairs write to the chairman stating the member's views and offering any sug- gestions which he believes will be useful in determining the proper course of action. The future of the system of regions and directors will stand or fall as the result of the present survey.

Write to John E. Galley, 1610 Holloway Avenue, Midland, Texas

* * * * * * * * * * * * * * * * * * *

PADRE ISLAND
by Dorothy Kerr, Corpus Christi

Padre Island is a long, narrow strip of sand, stretching from Corpus Christi Pass south to Brazos Santiago Pass at Port Isabel. It is a tall sand bar, being constantly built up by sand from the sea. To the east lie the blue waters of the Gulf of Mexico and to the west, the brownish, shallow, highly saline waters of Laguna Madre. The Intracoastal canal passes through the Laguna like a green-gray river.

Padre Island was named for Padre Nicolas Balli, who obtained it as a grant from Charles IV of Spain at the beginning of the 19th century. For many years he and his nephew, Juan Jose Balli, operated a rancho on the island and used it as a refuge on occasions when Mexico and Spain had differences of opinion.

It was known to the Spaniards as Isla Blanca; and White Island would still be a better name. It is a world of stark whiteness -- whirling white gulls and terns; water breaking itself into a white foam against the hard white sand; during the day bathed in the white hot sun and at night transformed into a magic land of white sand and water, laced by the silver filigree of the moonlight.

Padre Island is some 116 miles long. Together with the many smaller islands and spoil banks in the Laguna, it offers year-round haven to many species of birds. Generally the birds of Padre cannot be separated from those of the Laguna. Among the shore and water birds are white pelicans, brown pelicans, laughing gulls, white- faced glossy ibis, white ibis, royal, caspian, least and gull-billed terns, anhingas, black skimmers, spoonbills, sanderlings, willets, dowitchers, several sandpipers,

Wilson's plover, long-billed curlews, yellow legs, avocets and cormorants. Wild
turkeys cross over from King Ranch on the mainland.

     Countless species of water and land migratory birds stop over on the island
during their annual pilgramages. Loons, grebes, red-breasted mergansers, sandhill
cranes, both Mexican and double-crested cormorants, wood ibis, black terns, knots
and many more can be seen on the Gulf beach and in the sheltered bays on the Laguna
side. In the spring, warblers cross the Gulf of Mexico to Padre on their northern
migrations. Wave after wave of swallows, mourning doves, meadowlarks, scissortails,
blackbirds and even hummingbirds fly over. A never-to-be-forgotten experience is to
watch the thousands of swallows sweeping over the dunes and down the beach barely
clearing the ground and water; at times it seems impossible for them not to be washed under by a high wave. A most thrilling sight is to watch a magnificent frigate
bird come sailing down the wind on a pirate hunt for food.

     The white pelicans have their nesting grounds on South Bird Island in the
Laguna and in late spring and early summer months transform this little island
until, from the distance, it has the appearance of a snow bank. The island is
under the protection of the National Audubon Society. Prevailing southeast trade
winds, blowing across the Laguna from Padre, guard the nesting place from the coyotes
that inhabit Padre Island. The Laguna Madre white pelican colony is unique in two
respects: it is some 1400 miles southeast of its nearest neighboring colony in Great
Salt Lake, Utah, and it is the only colony nesting on an island surrounded by the
waters of the sea. Another bird of special interest nesting on South Bird Island is
the reddish egret in the white color phase. Also under the protection of the National
Audubon Society are Shamrock Point, Crane Island, North Bird Island, Green Island
and Three Islands in the lower Laguna.

     Other birds nesting on the island include black skimmers, herons, egrets,
grackles, quail, mockingbirds, scissortail flycatchers, nighthawks, red-winged
blackbirds, killdeer, cowbirds, horned larks and turkey vultures.

     In addition to coyotes, the animal life of the island consists mainly of
badgers, skunks, kangaroo rats and ground squirrels, opossum, pocket mice, pocket
gophers and jack rabbits in abundance. There are horned toads, snakes, fiddler
crabs, hermit crabs, edible blue crabs and countless number of "ghost" crabs or
sand crabs and sand lizards. At times loggerhead turtles come to the beaches from
the sea and, in season, Portugese man-of-war are washed onto the beach by the
thousands.

     The vegetation is semi-tropical with scores of flowering plants, clusters
of mesquite and scrub oak, prickly pear, crab grass, painted drop seed grass,
glass wort, sea lavender, seaside partride pea, stemodia, gaillardia or Indian
blanket, seaside evening primrose, sunflowers, Spanish dagger and dodder. Most
characteristic of the Island vegetation is the goat-foot morning glory vines
tracing patterns on the dunes and sea oats topping nearly every sand knoll.

     Shells found on the Island have been classified and number about 150
species and sub-species. A comprehensive display of these is on exhibit in the
Padre Island Museum. Shell collecting is best following a gulf storm or a norther
with high tides. Many beautiful and unusual shells may then be picked up along
the high tide line. Occasional lucky finds may be made at any time, of course,
both on the beach and behind the sand dunes and in the many passes where a previous

storm or high water has left them to bleach in the merciless sunshine. For the
most part, however, the ever-pounding surf grinds and pounds the shells along the
beach into countless fragments in the never-ending process of creating the sands
of Padre.

Hundreds of thousands of cocinas (or butterfly shells) dwell along the tide
line and come to the surface with each receding wave. Early Islanders made an
excellent and nourishing stew from these miniature clams, a habit still practiced
by the curious and adventurous.

During the last six years, two causeways have been constructed connecting
the Island with the mainland. One is at Corpus Christi and the other at Port
Isabel. Millions of people have crossed these structures, but comparatively few
motorists have driven the entire length of the island. The tides and winds are
erratic and at times the water covers the beach to the white dunes that run almost
the length of the island. The trip is not safe for passenger cars. At Big Shell
and Little Shell (shell reefs about half way down the island) the pounding surf
throws up millions of shells. These never pack and are shifted with each new tide.
Fishing is excellent here, but the beach is treacherous, and automobiles are stranded and deserted frequently enough to serve as a warning to those who would venture
there.

Padre Island could (and should) become one of the greatest wildlife refuges
on the North American continent and a Park of nation-wide attraction.

* * * * * * * * * * * * * * *

OFFICERS, REGIONAL DIRECTORS, AND COMMITTEE CHAIRMEN

President:	Dr. Clarence Cottam, Box 1396, Sinton
Vice-President:	Warren M. Pulich, 2021 Rosebud, Irving
Secretary-Treasurer:	Miss Carrie Holcomb, 1008 Missouri, Houston 6
Corresponding Secretary:	Kent Rylander, NTSC Station, Box 5305, Denton
Editor:	Mrs. J. W. LeSassier, 1611 W. Indiana, Midland
Past-President:	John E. Galley, 1610 Holloway Avenue, Midland

Region I: Mrs. I. D. Acord, 1911 Cherry Street, Amarillo
Region II: Mrs. Mike O'Neil, 1311 Bonham Street, Commerce
Region III: George K. Stephenson, Box 276, North Street Station, Nacogdoches
Region IV: Harold L Williams, Route 2, Box 45-B, Midland
Region V: Philip Campbell III, 1510 Forest Trail, Austin 3
Region VI: Dr. Cornelia Smith, Biology Dept., Baylor University, Waco
Region VII: A. Earl Jourde, 1017 Stirman Street, Corpus Christi
Region VIII: L.A.M. Barnette, 4801 Linden, Bellaire

Library:	Mrs. Norma Oates, 5908 Charlotte, Houston 5
Conservation:	Armand Yramategui, 2520 Calumet, Houston 4
Membership-Publicity:	Warren Pulich, 2021 Rosebud, Irving
Nominating:	Mrs. Harold L Williams, Route 2, Box 45-B, Midland
Constitution and By-laws:	John E. Galley, 1610 Holloway Avenue, Midland

DATE 8-24-56 FRI TRIP NUMBER 1.
STARTING TIME 5:30 p.m. WITH WHOM: Bob, Don,
RETURN TIME 4:30 a.m. Sat. BARB, GERTIE, JOHN JENNINGS
LOCALITY VISITED: COPANO WEATHER FAIR
BAY AT MISSION BAY WIND: AMT. STRONG
TOTAL SPECIES SEEN ____ DIRECTION DUE EAST
NEW SPECIES: NONE. TEMPERATURE 80
First time to record: HUMIDITY DAMP
* FORSTER'S TERN CLOUDS: thin but ALL OVER JUST PAST FULL MOON
* UPLAND PLOVER TIDES:

NUMBER:	SPECIES:	REMARKS —
	BL. TERNS	HAWKING OVER FIELDS
100	"	SIT SALT FLATS
6-8	FORSTER'S T. ♀	SOME W. BL. TERNS
* 1.	UPLAND PLOVER	IN PLOWED FIELD
1.	BL. BELLED PLOVER	" "
	MORNING DOVES	ROADSIDE
	BOAT-T. GRACKLE	"
4	MEADOW LARKS	"
2	JUV. GT. BLUES	NEST - MISSION BAY
		ABLE TO FLY ABOUT TREES
1	AM EGRET	ROOKERY - MISSION BAY
6	BLACK SKIMMERS up and down beach	X "

John + Bub eat trot lines.
Kids and I bedded - down

9-8-56 COOL FRONT
MARYLAND (1347 (?) Drive CC

YELLOW-BR. CHATS ALL PLENTIFUL
HUMMERS
FLY CATCHERS

HAVE BEEN WATCHING
MARS EACH NIGHT
— COMES UP RIGHT
IN FRONT DOOR.
TONIGHT — WHEN IT IS
CLOSEST TO EARTH
& HAZE OBSTRUCTED
IT NEARLY ALL
EVENING.

Jan. 22nd.

First robin noon in yard.
Lots of starlings. One flock of
over a hundred at Armory.

Feb. 2nd. a.m.

Watched sparrow hawk swoop down
from light wire & capture small
animal on ground — probably a
mouse.   Baldwin blvd.

Noon — unidentified singer in back
yard. Gone when I got
binocs. Reminiscent of Painted
Bunting but not quite right.
2 or 3 appox. flycatchers in yard.

Feb. 3rd.   Early a.m. to noon — flocks of
starlings all over town. Here
to church to Southside to
Filter Center and back by
Baldwin blvd.

DATE: Sat. Feb. 16, 1957   TRIP NUMBER 2

STARTING TIME: 1 p.m.   WITH WHOM: C.C.O.C.

RETURN TIME: 7 p.m.

LOCALITY VISITED WELDER

WILDLIFE REFUGE, SINTON,   WEATHER Misty — OVERCAST — COOL

TEXAS, DESTINATION: WIND: AMT. At 15-25mph — VERY GUSTY
                              GUSTS TO 30

Drove over entire refuge. DIRECTION No. & No. EAST

Dr. Clarence Cottam, Guide TEMPERATURE 60s
and Speaker.

TOTAL SPECIES: HUMIDITY

NEW SPECIES: CLOUDS Low — heavy — Main clouds

Sennet's White Tailed   MOON

Hawk (2 prs)   TIDES

FIRST TIME LISTED: Sand Hill Cranes

Number	Species	Remarks —
At Least Doz.	Sp. Hawk	On wires along roadside on way up.
Several	Shrike	
1	Loon	Causeway ditto. above.
	Meadow Larks	
On Refuge		
Many flocks	Turkey	Very plentiful —
	Deer	Ditto. Few bucks.
1	Kingfisher	On river bank
Many	Lark sp.	

NUMBER	SPECIES	REMARKS —
FLOCK	STARLING	SITTING ON DEAD TREE AT DUSK.
	MARSH HAWKS	PLENTIFUL
FLOCK (ABT 50)	SANDHILL CRANES	FLEW OVER
	SENNET'S	
2 (PRS.)	WH-TAIL. HAWKS	LOOKING FOR NESTING SITE
(1	BALD EAGLE NEST)	
	CARDINAL	
	MOCKERS	
AB2 2 DOC.	KILLDEER	
	MEADOW LARKS	
	SP. HAWKS	
	T. BUZZARDS	
(1	RABBIT	)
(	PACK RAT DENS	MANY)
2	CARACARA	

WEATHER
Today—Cooler   Sailing—Rough
Yesterday's High and Low
CofC 81-69   Airport 83-63
Sunrise 7:07 a.m.   Set 6:22 p.m.
Moonrise 8:56 p.m.   Set 8:13 a.m.
High Tide 5:10 p.m.   Low 10:44 a.m.
                      11:06 p.m.

Cooler Weather Predicted Here

Weather Map on Page 12A

A shadow of winter will return to Corpus Christi and the area today, the Weather Bureau said, with temperatures due to dip to the 60s.

North and northeast winds of 15-25 miles an hour, with gusts up to 30 miles an hour are on tap, with the high temperature today and tomorrow predicted at 62-66 degrees. The low tonight will be 46-50 degrees.

The winds will become northeast and east at 10-15 miles an hour tonight. Tomorrow they will be mostly easterly at 12-18 miles an hour.

Small craft warnings will go up.

2-23-57   yard (Maryland) myrtle warbler
                 St

3.1.57   "   "   "

3.6.57   "   "   " drank
                              from pan on picnic table

3.7.57   "   robin   (6:30 a.m.
                              barely dawn

3.16.57   "   blue gray gnatcatcher
                                      all day

3-19-57   <u>singing</u> in   kinglet
              Longuenilla 7:30 a.m.

3-26-57 noon Myrtle ♂ flycatching from
                  hackberry tree

DATE: MAR. 3 - 1957   TRIP NO.   57-3

STARTING TIME: 6:30 a.m.   WITH WHOM: C.C.O.C.

RETURN TIME: LEFT AT 3 p.m. BOB, BARBIE, GERTIE,

LOCALTY VISITED: AUSTWELL; LODE, TOWNSEND, SEATON,
                                  CLARK, GETZENDANER,
ARANSAS GAME REFUGE, ————————
                      (BYNUM, Dr. ASHER, ————)
BLACKJACK PENESULA.   WEATHER: FOG 6:30 a.m.-
                      BALMY
GUIDE: MR.   LARD   FOG LIFTING 8:15   RAIN ON
                      OVERCAST ALL DAY   RETURN
TOT. SPEC. SEEN; 56   WIND: AMT.   STILL
    23 OFF; 33 ON REFUGE
NEW SPEC: DIRECTION

PR. CHICKEN   TEMP.   64 AUSTWELL

                           HUMIDITY - W. of N.

                           CLOUDS - OVERCAST

                           ARRIVE   9:30

NUMBER	SPEC.	REMARKS	
	KINGFISHER •	WIRE BY CAUSEWAY	7 a.m.
	L. BLUES	CAUSEWAY	
	SHRIKE •		
	SP. HAWKS •		
	B.T. GRACKLES		
	R. TERN •		
	RB GULL •		

(facing page:)

ᴴᴴᴴ ҇

???

(24 mi - bayside
to C.C.)

DATE: MAR. 3 - 1957 TRIP NO. 57-3

STARTING TIME: 6:30 a.m. WITH WHOM: C.C.O.C.

RETURN TIME: LEFT at 3p.m. BOB. BARBIE, GERTIE.

LOCALTY VISITED: AUSTWELL; LODGE. TOWNSEND, SEATON

ARANSAS GAME REFUGE, CLARK, GETZENDANER,

BLACKJACK PENESULA. (BYNUM, Dr. ASHER, ——)

WEATHER: FOG 6:30 a.m. - BALMY

GUIDE: MR. LARD FOG LIFTING 8:15 LT. RAIN ON RETURN

OVER CAST ALL DAY

TOT. SPEC. SEEN; 56 WIND: AMT. STILL

23 off; 33 ON REFUGE

NEW SPEC: DIRECTION

PR. CHICKEN

TEMP. 64 AUSTWELL

HUMIDITY - W. of N.

CLOUDS - OVERCAST

ARRIVE 9:30

NUMBER	SPEC.	REMARKS
1	KINGFISHER •	WIRE BY CAUSEWAY 7 a.m.
	L. BLUES	CAUSEWAY
	SHRIKE •	
	SP. HAWKS	
	BO.T. GRACKLES	
	R. TERN •	
	RB GULL •	
	MOCKER	
	M. DOVE	
2	LB. CURLEW	SALT MARSH NO. of ARANSAS PASS

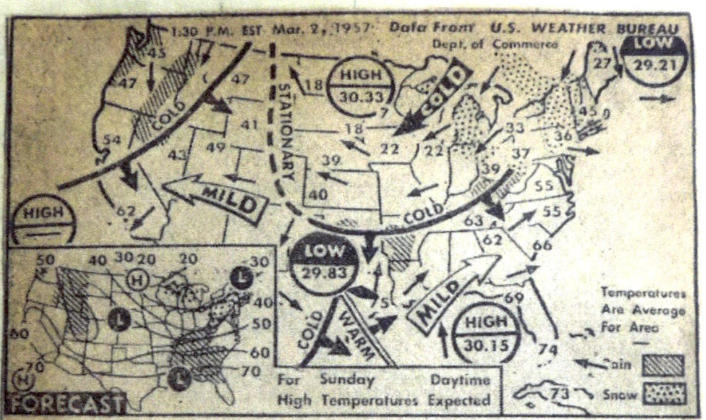

WEATHER BUREAU FORECAST—Snow flurries are forecast for northern New England, the north and central Appalachians and parts of the Great Lakes area today. Rain is expected from the Tennessee Valley south to northern Florida and the central Gulf states. Showers also are forecast for the north and central Rockies, the Cascades and Washington Coast. It will be warmer in the north and central Plains regions. (AP Wirephoto Map)

TABLE OF GULF TIDES

	High		Low	
Today	4:27 a.m.	4:41 p.m.	10:24 a.m.	10:27 p.m.
Monday	5:22 a.m.	4:59 p.m.	10:58 a.m.	11:04 p.m.
Tuesday	6:21 a.m.	5:10 p.m.	11:37 a.m.	11:46 p.m.
Wednesday	7:31 a.m.	5:06 p.m.	12:19 p.m.	
Thursday	8:49 a.m.	4:43 p.m.	12:35 a.m.	1:14 p.m.
Friday	10:14 a.m.		1:33 a.m.	
Saturday	11:30 a.m.		2:40 a.m.	

Scattered Rains Predicted Here

3-3-57

Weather Map on Page 12A

A few widely scattered showers are predicted in the area today by the Weather Bureau. Mild temperatures are expected through tomorrow.

The high today and tomorrow will be 72-76 degrees with the mercury dropping to 60-64 degrees tonight.

Winds early today will be southeasterly east at 12-18 miles an hour. This afternoon they will become easterly to northeasterly at the same speed. Tomorrow winds will be mostly east at 12-18 miles an hour.

The forecast for South Texas: Partly cloudy with widely scattered showers Sunday and Monday, cooler Sunday.

WEATHER

Today—Mild Sailing—Favorable
Yesterday's High and Low
CofC 77-67 Airport 80-63
Sunrise 6:52 a.m. Set 6:32 p.m.
Moonrise 7:42 a.m. Set 8:31 p.m.
High Tide 4:27 a.m. Low 10:24 p.m.
4:41 p.m.

3-3-57

Solunar Tables

The schedule of Solunar Periods, as printed below, has been taken from John Alden Knight's SOLUNAR TABLES. Plan your days so that you will be fishing in good territory or hunting in good cover during these times. If you wish to find the best sport that each day has to offer.

The Major Periods are shown in boldface type. These begin at the times shown and last for an hour and a half or two hours thereafter. The Minor Periods, shown in regular type, are of somewhat shorter duration.

March		A.M.		P.M.	
3	Sunday	7:06	12:55	7:30	1:30
4	Monday	7:45	1:35	8:10	2:00
5	Tuesday	8:30	2:20	8:50	2:40
6	Wednesday	9:15	3:05	9:35	3:25
7	Thursday	10:00	3:50	10:25	4:15
8	Friday	10:50	4:40	11:15	5:05
9	Saturday	11:45	5:35	— —	6:00

About 10 p.m, after visiting rookery. — No birds, few am. egrets and fair. gr. blues still in trees — all others gone. Fishermen camped right in rookery? Saw few birds back in marshes. Planned to go have a look at 5 am. tomorrow [set alarm]. Coming over Bob, Gertie & I saw 2 birds against sun — size of cardinals & with top-nots — but a chirping scolding note quite unlike cardinal — at water hole. Bob, John & Don had come over in Jeep & the girls & I had chevy. Planned to go to water hole EARLY tomorrow — how little I knew that I would be up at 4 a.m! Bob & Gertie woke me up — Said it looked like rain! Boy! Such a cloud! and did we ever pack & get out in a hurry! If you're caught in those flats in a rain, you stay there! Hard shower by the time we reached the shell road. Home at 6 a.m. ate breakfast. girls went back to sleep. Bob, John & Don went back in Jeep to rescue our tent lines & I cleaned house. Wouldn't let Smoky in — so he is setting on the back steps talking to himself.

NO. DOZ	SPEC.	REM.
1, 4	MEADOWLARK, PRARIE	ABU. ROCKPORT
	QUAIL .	
2 M. NOT 2 DOZ	Pr. CHICKENS .	ABT 15
	COWBIRDS	TIVOLI
1	REDWING .	BY CATTLE TANK
1	KILLDEER .	RAN ACROSS RD.
	MARSH HAWK	REFUGE RD.
Gbt. dec.	COWBIRDS	UNDER FEET OF 2 COWS
	~~CARACARA~~	FLEW
	Ł HAWK UNID	~~BRG-HAWR~~ BRT.
		GR. BLUE HERON
	CARACARA 1	SITTING IN FIELD - WLK AROUND
		FEEDING — THEN FLEW
	SWALLOWS	~~STARLINGS~~ UNID.
3 2	BL. VUL	
	FLICKERS	
	ALEGATOR	
	AM. EGRETS	
	GR. BLUE	
	BL-N. STILT	
	YELLOWLEGS	
	SNOWY	
	REDDISH	
	GR. BL. L. BL.	
	T. VULTURE	
	BL. SKIMMERS	
	WILLETS	

5. 4. 2017

NO. DOZ	SPEC.	REM.
1, 4	MEADOWLARK, PRARIE	ABU. ROCKPORT
	QUAIL .	
2 M. NOT 2 DOZ	Pr. CHICKENS .	ABT 15
	COWBIRDS	TIVOLI
1	REDWING .	BY CATTLE TANK
1	KILLDEER .	RAN ACROSS RD.
	MARSH HAWK	REFUGE RD.
Gbt. dec.	COWBIRDS	UNDER FEET OF 2 COWS
	~~CARACARA~~	FLEW
	Ł HAWK UNID	~~BRG-HAWR~~ BRT.
		GR. BLUE HERON
	CARACARA 1	SITTING IN FIELD - WLK AROUND
		FEEDING — THEN FLEW
	SWALLOWS	~~STARLINGS~~ UNID.
3 2	BL. VUL	
	FLICKERS	
	ALEGATOR	
	AM. EGRETS	
	GR. BLUE	
	BL-N. STILT	
	YELLOWLEGS	
	SNOWY	
	REDDISH	
	GR. BL. L. BL.	
	T. VULTURE	
	BL. SKIMMERS	
	WILLETS	

5. 4. 2017

NO.	SPEC.	REM.
DDRS		
1,4	MEADOWLARK · PRARIE	ABU. ROCKPORT
	QUAIL ·	
2 M.	PR. CHICKENS ·	ABT 15
NOT 2 DOZ	COWBIRDS	TIVOLI
1	REDWING ·	BY CATTLE TANK
1	KILLDEER ·	RAN ACROSS RD.
	MARSH HAWK	REFUGE RD.
6bt-dac.	COWBIRDS	UNDEFEET OF 2 COWS
	~~CARACARA~~	FLEW
	Lt HAWK UNID. ~~BAG-HAWK~~ BRT.	
	GR. BLUE HERON	
	CARACARA 1	SITTING IN FIELD · WLK AROUND
		FEEDING — THEN FLEW
	SWALLOWS	~~STARLINGS~~ UNID.
3 a	BL. UUL	
	FLICKERS	
	ALEGATOR	
	AM. EGRETS	
	GR. BLUE	
	BL-N. STILT	
	YELLOW LEGS	
	SNOWY	
	REDDISH	
	GR. BL. L. BL.	
	T. VULTURE	
	BL. SKIMMERS	
	WILLETS	
	WH PELICANS	
	CARDINALS	

(33)

	PACK RAT DEN	
	BLUE JAY	
	L.B. CURLEW	
	CANADA GEESE	
	LEAST TERN / SHRIKE / SP. HAWKS	
50	SNOW GOOSE	2 BLUE GEESE
8	CORMORANTS / DOVE, M / GODWIT	
11	chipping sp.	
2	Turkey hens	
3 rafts	cormorants	in 3 rafts composing alt. 75 birds
1	CORMORANT	CAUSEWAY — RAIN
	DUCKS	fly n RAIN
	TERNS	FISHING IN RAIN
LRG RAFTS ~~DUCKS~~	DUCKS	
	GULLS, TERNS	
	HERONS, EGRETS	
	SHORE BIRDS	IK BAYS, COVES, FULTON BEACH COVE.

DATE   MAR. 17, 1957   TRIP # 57-4

STARTING TIME: 1:30 p.m.   WITH WHOM: BOB, BIRDIE,
ARRIVED: GERTIE
RETURN TIME:

LOCALITY VISITED: ARANSAS   WEATHER: OVERCAST, COOL
    NAT'L WILDLIFE REFUGE   WIND: ANT   GUSTS 20 to 30
                               DIRECTION: S.E.
                               TEMP. 70-84
                               HUMIDITY

NUMBER   SPEC.   REMARKS

1 BL. NECK STILT   ROCKPORT
SEV. RAFTS DUCKS   "
      SR. HAWKS   ON WIRES   NO. OF ROCKPORT
      SHRIKE   "   "   "

4 MARSH HAWKS

   CORMORANTS   BAY CAUSEWAY   SEV. SPP.

   MEADOWLARK   IN BLOOM.

   KILLDEER   BY ROADSIDE   WINE CUPS, PRICKLY POPPY

                                     PRIMROSE, SW. WILLIAM

   ON REFUGE: PHLOX, BLUE BONNET

      BLUE JAY HEARD AT NOOTRI. IN-EV. SUSAN, THISTLE
1 TURKEY HEN IN MIDDLE OF ROAD, NOT FRIGHTENED, NOT INCLINED TO MOVE.
2 WHOOPERS FEEDING ABT 1½ mi. FROM TOWER.
2 ROSEATE SPOONBILLS ALTO (MATURE - SHOCKING PINK)
3 AM. EGRETS
100 or so WHITE PELICANS ; 3 BR. PELICANS
FEW GR. BLUES
3 REDDISH EGRETS - MANY, MANY OWLS VULTURES
   SOARING ON HWY BACK TOWARD KINGPORT

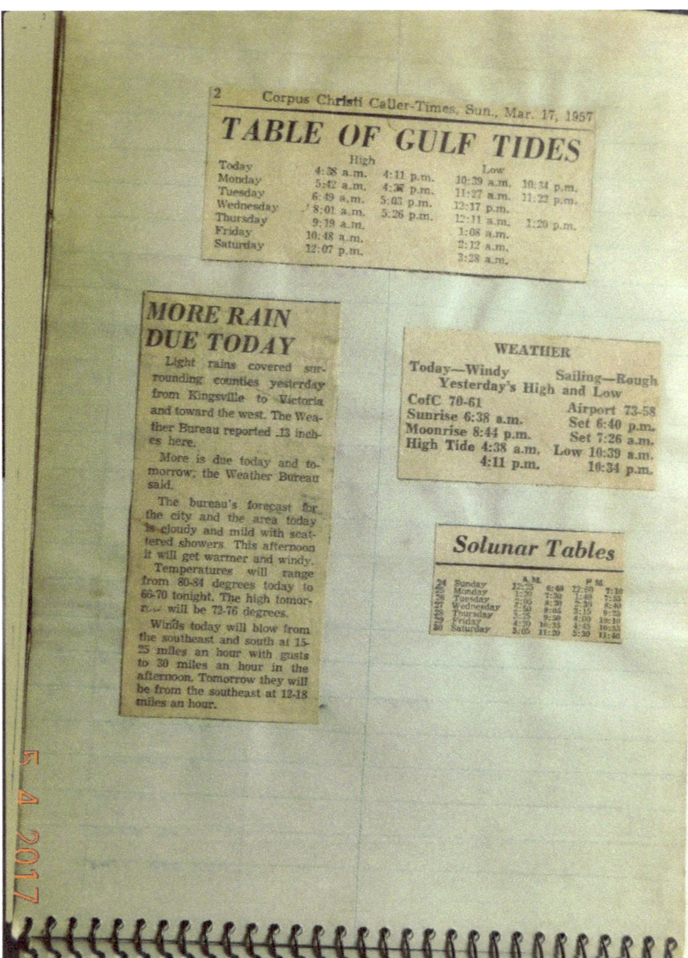

TABLE OF GULF TIDES

	High		Low	
Today	4:38 a.m.	4:11 p.m.	10:39 a.m.	10:34 p.m.
Monday	5:42 a.m.	4:36 p.m.	11:27 a.m.	11:22 p.m.
Tuesday	6:49 a.m.	5:03 p.m.	12:17 p.m.	
Wednesday	8:01 a.m.	5:26 p.m.	12:11 a.m.	1:20 p.m.
Thursday	9:19 a.m.		1:08 a.m.	
Friday	10:48 a.m.		2:12 a.m.	
Saturday	12:07 p.m.		3:28 a.m.	

MORE RAIN DUE TODAY

Light rains covered surrounding counties yesterday from Kingsville to Victoria and toward the west. The Weather Bureau reported .13 inches here.

More is due today and tomorrow, the Weather Bureau said.

The bureau's forecast for the city and the area today is cloudy and mild with scattered showers. This afternoon it will get warmer and windy.

Temperatures will range from 80-84 degrees today to 66-70 tonight. The high tomorrow will be 72-76 degrees.

Winds today will blow from the southeast and south at 15-25 miles an hour with gusts to 30 miles an hour in the afternoon. Tomorrow they will be from the southeast at 12-18 miles an hour.

WEATHER

Today—Windy   Sailing—Rough
Yesterday's High and Low
CofC 70-61   Airport 73-58
Sunrise 6:38 a.m.   Set 6:40 p.m.
Moonrise 8:44 p.m.   Set 7:26 a.m.
High Tide 4:38 a.m. Low 10:39 a.m.
         4:11 p.m.   10:34 p.m.

Solunar Tables

	A.M.		P.M.	
24 Sunday	12:35	6:40	12:40	7:10
25 Monday	1:25	7:30	1:40	7:55
26 Tuesday	2:00	8:30	2:20	8:40
27 Wednesday	2:50	9:10	3:15	9:25
28 Thursday	3:30	9:50	4:00	10:15
29 Friday	4:30	10:35	4:45	10:55
30 Saturday	5:05	11:20	5:30	11:40

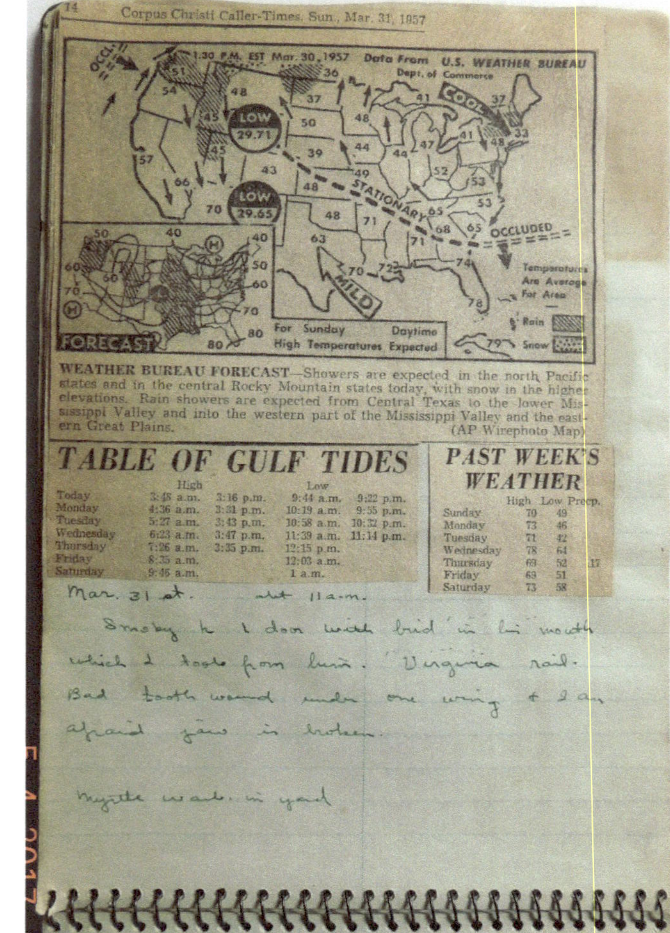

WEATHER BUREAU FORECAST—Showers are expected in the north Pacific states and in the central Rocky Mountain states today, with snow in the higher elevations. Rain showers are expected from Central Texas to the lower Mississippi Valley and into the western part of the Mississippi Valley and the eastern Great Plains. (AP Wirephoto Map)

TABLE OF GULF TIDES

	High		Low	
Today	3:48 a.m.	3:16 p.m.	9:44 a.m.	9:22 p.m.
Monday	4:36 a.m.	3:31 p.m.	10:19 a.m.	9:55 p.m.
Tuesday	5:27 a.m.	3:43 p.m.	10:58 a.m.	10:32 p.m.
Wednesday	6:23 a.m.	3:47 p.m.	11:39 a.m.	11:14 p.m.
Thursday	7:26 a.m.	3:35 p.m.	12:15 p.m.	
Friday	8:35 a.m.		12:03 a.m.	
Saturday	9:46 a.m.		1 a.m.	

PAST WEEK'S WEATHER

	High	Low	Precp.
Sunday	70	49	
Monday	73	46	
Tuesday	71	42	
Wednesday	78	64	
Thursday	68	52	.17
Friday	63	51	
Saturday	73	58	

Mar. 31 at.   abt 11 a.m.

Smoky h I door with bird in his mouth which I took from him. Virginia rail. Bad tooth wound under one wing & I am afraid jaw is broken.

Myrtle warb. in yard

Date.   Mar. 31, 1957   Im   Trip   No. 575
Starting time 1:00   With whom: To meet
arrival   2:00   Bob, Don, Brownie,
Locality visited: Goose Island   Mildred who camped
State Park - Big Tree   at big tree last night.
WEATHER: Showers
Fulton Beach 11:30 few   (rained all & no more to 10 p.m.)
forecast.
Gr. Blues - 1 small raft   Wind: 50 ½ S.W. 15-25
Ducks.   6:30 p.m. Bl.   Temp: 88°
Skimmers, few gulls sitting
up close to road.   Bull thistles,
Blue bonnets, phlox, primrose
Big Tree: Took Mr. Rail's pix   and prickly poppy - great carpets of these.
½ Don turned him loose   Tiny white daisy - chappel
close to water ie   flower. Coral bean in
Mesquite thicket.   bloom. Coreopsis.
Scissor tail migration.
Swallows. Cardinals
in full song. Male
Painted Bunting.

Small Craft Warnings Due

Scattered thundershowers with strong shifting winds that may make sailing dangerous are predicted for this evening by the Weather Bureau.

The bureau said small craft warnings may be hoisted later today because of the wind shift. Temperatures will range from a high of 78-82 degrees to a low tonight of 58-62. The high tomorrow will be 66-70 degrees.

Winds today will be south and southwest at 15-25 miles an hour, shifting to northerly winds at 20 miles an hour tonight. Tomorrow the winds will blow from the north and northeast at 12-18 miles an hour.

WEATHER

Today—Showers   Sailing—Choppy
Yesterday's High and Low

CofC 71-64	Airport 73-58
Sunrise 6:22 a.m.	Set 6:47 p.m.
Moonrise 6:18 a.m.	Set 7:20 p.m.
High Tide 3:38 a.m.	Low 9:44 a.m.
3:16 p.m.	9:22 p.m.

Solunar Tables

By John Alden Knight

First Whooping Cranes Leave On Spring Flight to Canada

4-17-57

Caller-Times News Service

AUSTWELL — Eight of the 23 whooping cranes which wintered on Aransas National Wildlife Refuge have departed for the summer in northwestern Canada, Refuge Manager Claude Lard said today. An aerial survey of the refuge was made yesterday.

The spring migration is about on schedule, perhaps a little late, as usually about half the colony are gone by April 14. On a few occasions some have lingered in South Texas into May.

The family of three who fed around Mustang Lake, in sight from a tower on the refuge, are among those who have left. Lard said. Thirteen are still on the refuge and two are on Matagorda Island. The status of one who wintered on Laureles Ranch is not known.

MIGRATION NOTES

4-15-57 Mo.
7 am.   INVASION.
b.g. gnatcatcher
KENTUCKY WARB.
BELL'S VIREO ?
5 p.m.
  YLO. WARB.
  MALE HUMMERS at
  BOUGANVILLA ALL DAY.

4-16.
7am. redstart ♂
BALTIMORE ORIOLE ♂
THRUSH (UNID.)
b.g gnatcatcher
5:30 pm.
  MEX. CHAT.

4-17
6:30   (yd. full)
HUMMERS ♂
B. ORIOLE ♂ & ♀
Yb cuckoo
Ken. warb.

4-18
ON OHIO ST. Summer
TANAGER. abt 8:30 am.
Blucher Park noon
Md ylo throat
red start ♂
Inca doves bldg n.s
6 am.
4-19 nighthawk

4-21 Summer TANAGER
ENG SP. BABIES
IN PALM TREE
4-25 CATBIRDS   (Bayside Day Camp: warblers, catbirds, flycatchers)
4-24 - NIGHTHAWKS - HAWKING IN THE RAIN. 6:30-7:00 am
4-30 Warbler mig. (rain)
ASH THROATED crested Flycatcher
BALTIMORE ORIOLE ♂
REDSTART ♂
SWALLOW mig — Some so low nearly skimming house tops — dodging wires as they go

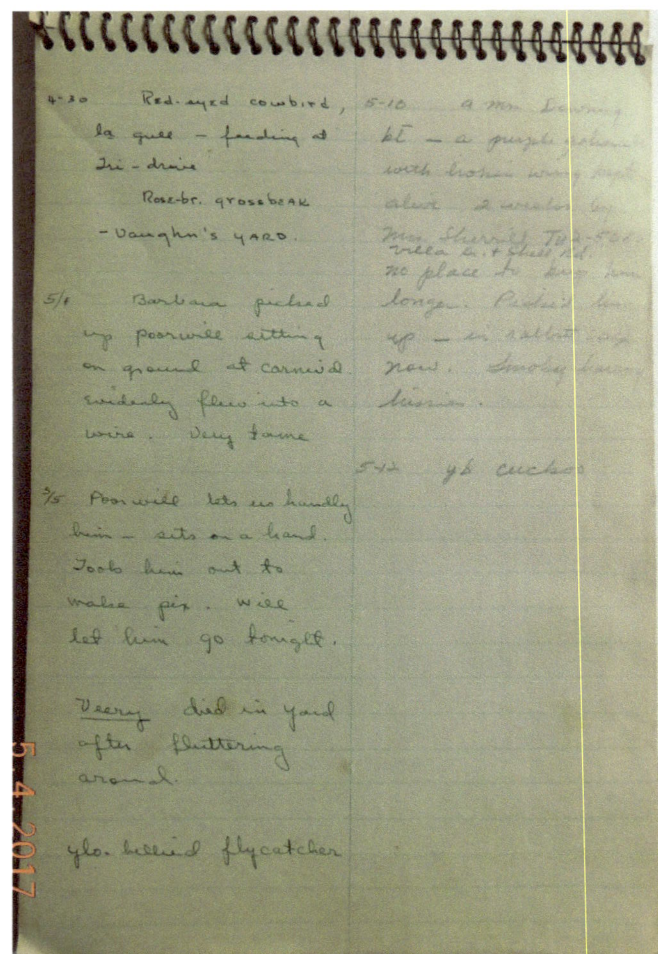

4-30   Red-eyed cowbird,
        La gull — feeding at
        Tri-drive
           Rose-br. grosbeak
        - Vaughn's yard.

5/1   Barbara picked
        up poorwill sitting
        on ground at carwash
        evidently flew into a
        wire. Very tame

7/5   Poorwill lets us handle
        him — sits on a hand.
        Took him out to
        make pix. Will
        let him go tonight.

        Veery died in yard
        after fluttering
        around.

        ylo. billed flycatcher

5-10   a mn Downy
        bk — a purple [illegible]
        with broken wing [illegible]
        alive 2 weeks by
        Mrs. Sherrill 782-5[illegible]
        Villa [illegible] + shell rd
        no place to keep him
        longer. Picked him
        up — in rabbit cage
        now. Smoky brown
        lesion.

5-12   yb cuckoo

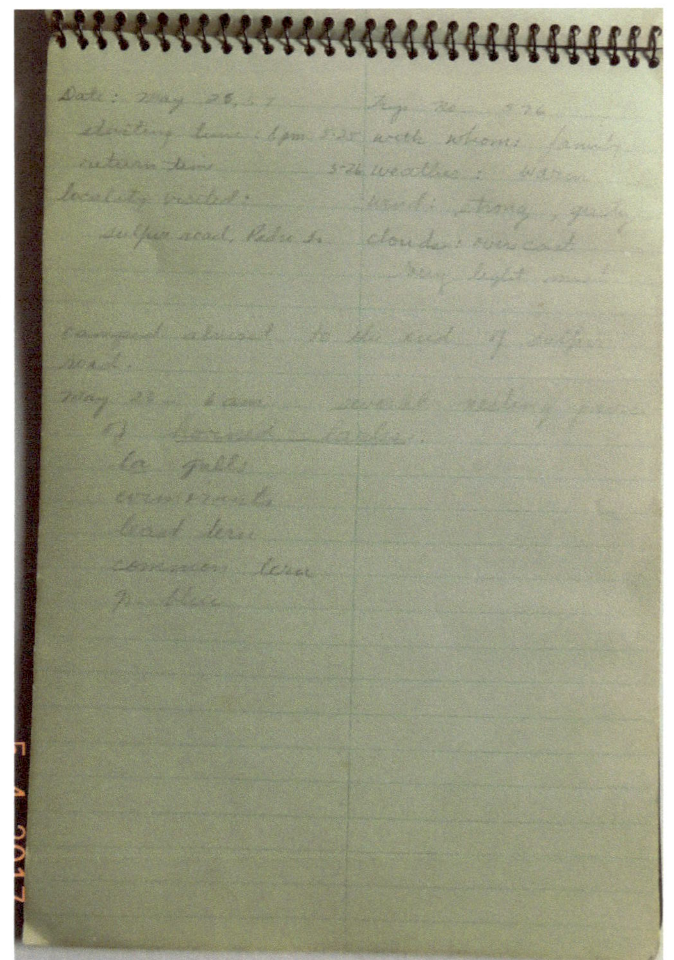

Date: May 28, 5[illegible]   Tryp [illegible] 5-26
starting time 6pm 5-25   with whom: family
return time   5-26   weather: Warm
locality visited: wind: strong, gusty
    sulphur road, Padre [illegible]   clouds: overcast
                     very light [illegible]

campout almost to the end of sulphur
road.
May 28 — 6am — several resting [illegible]
    of [illegible] tackle.
    La gulls
    cormorants
    least tern
    common tern
    m blue [illegible]

Primitive Unit   Camp Green Hill   July 7-20

<u>Bird Calendar</u>   kept by troop.
     (all verified by Kerr)
Cardinal   7-7   first day seen
Mockingbird
Carolina wren   scissor tail m & fem. 7-15
cuckoo   7-8   Fr. blue heron
Poorwill   bl. grey gnatcatcher
mourning dove   squirrel
Golden-fr. woodpecker   nighthawk   7-16
Inca dove   warbler feeding
laughing gull   baby cowbird   7-19
cowbird
vultures   7-9
least terns
orchard oriole   7-10
Mex. fly catcher
Eng. sparrow (at cafe)
Cardinal nest (2 young) 7-11
Chaparral cock
lark sparrow   7-12
water turkey   7-14

DATE: AUG 14-57   TRIP #   57P
LOCALITY VISITED: COPANO BAY-   WITH WHOM: BOB, DON
        MISSION BAY ROOKERY

NUMBER   SPEC.   REMARKS
          BLACK SKIMMERS
2   CURLEWS
abt 75   R. SPOONBILLS   ADULT & IM. IN MARSH 2:30pm
          TRI-COLOR, SPOONBILLS COUNTLESS BIRDS AT ROOKERY
          GR. BLUES, GRACKLES
          SNOWIES, AM. EGRETS
                           3:30 p.m.
25   WOOD IBIS   FEEDING & RESTING IN MARSH
                           3:35 MAN & DOG WALKED
                           THRU - ALARMING BIRDS -
                           SOME FLEW. SOME SETTLED
                           BACK DOWN,
                           7:45 p.m. COMET SITED
                           TUST BELOW BIG
                           DIPPER, FORMING ICE
                           CREAM CONE WITH
                           BOWL
AUG. 16   5:30 a.m.   DROVE TOWARD ROOKERY
                           STOPPING ABOUT 100' AWAY.
                           HUNDREDS OF BIRDS IN MARSH
                           TO LEFT OF ROAD. OVER

July 31st - Aug 2nd.
Bob & I drove inland alone
to big shell - fishing poor.
weather hot & windy.
usual birds: lt. terns
                2 ducks in edge
blew teals   9 surf with flocks
                of terns.
                skimmers
                Caspian terns
                Willets
                var. sandpipers, etc

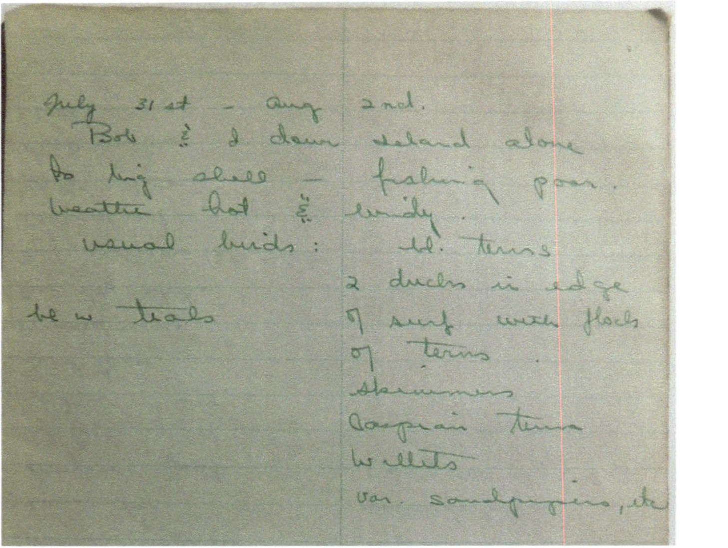

DATE: Aug 14-57   Trip #   578
LOCALITY VISITED: COPANO BAY - WITH WHOM? DOIS, DON
        MISSION BAY ROOKERY

NUMBER	SPEC.	REMARKS
	BLACK SKIMMERS	
2	CURLEWS	
abt 75	R. SPOONBILLS	ADULT & IM. IN MARSH 2:30pm
	TRI-COLOR, SPOONBILLS	COUNTLESS BIRDS AT ROOKERY
	GR BLUES, GRACKLES	
	SNOWIES, AM. EGRETS	
25	WOOD IBIS	3:30 p.m. FEEDING & RESTING IN MARSH

3:35 MAN & dog WALKED
THRU - ALARMING BIRDS -
SOME FLEW. SOME SETTLED
BACK DOWN.
7:45 p.m. COMET SITED
JUST BELOW BIG
DIPPER, forming ICE
CREAM CONE WITH
BOWL

AUG. 16   5:30 a.m.   DROVE TOWARD ROOKERY
STOPPING ABOUT 100' AWAY.
Hundreds of birds in MARSH
TO LEFT of road. OUT

11:30 am.

Dr. J. E. Bauer
Capano Sportsman Club
Refuge. Box 615
and Andy Brightman
went into rookery to
check nest & young
birds then down to talk
to us. Dr. Bauer is
trying to get Audubon
protection for rookery —

Dr. Bauer threw beer can down in camp.

1:30 pm.

Cliff swallows flitting over singly
la. gulls, least terns
common terns all active

5:30 — 6:45   Sat under gran pino
shrub close to rookery
— found night heron young still on
nests — also reddish egret (adult
& young)   Spoonbills flew over low
and tri-coloreds landed in bushes
not 15 feet away & sat there for
30 minutes just looking at me
— 3 of them - (people- watching, I guess)

---

300 in one compact group
— others scattered over a sq.
mile in various size groups
— some alone

Snowies, tri colored, spoonbills, gr. blues, wood ibis,
am. egrets & grackles   all scrambled up together.

over 100   wh. pelicans   way off to the west in
marsh alone ¾ a mile
from other birds.

Hundreds more in the
rookery and in edge of
water.   & passerines
— looks like cowbirds from
here.

cow birds (?)
laughing gulls
black skimmers
least terns   over the water.

water calm — little
wind. Sky clear,
little patches of
cumulus near
horizon.

6:45 pm. back at camp.

25-5-26   white pelicans — flocks flew over from north to settle in the far marshes.
Orange & navy jeep station wagon (Hillis Refugio, Westinghouse dealer) parked in rookery. (this car returned next morning and three times during next day — also following evening) flocks of them over marshes.

blacks terns

7:30 pm.   Birds by the hundreds flowing into the marshes and the rookery — shrubs are white with them — flock after from from all directions except East our Copano. Sun is down, sky tinged with pink & mauve — very small whispy, blue. gray clouds — Very windy.

least terns   from our Copano
23 white pelicans from main direction
4 willets   — more least terns.
Herons shifting constantly from marsh to rookery & back. 13 willets abt 25 feet from camp in edge of water — certainly feeding and watching me too.
7:30   almost dark — and still the birds come — as far as you can see with 8x40s — Snowies + tri-colors mostly come in low. Pelicans + gr. blues come in high then drop abruptly (most are now from the direction of the river to the north)

7:35 pm. Willets still nervously feeding. Herons + egrets literally flowing in from marshes to rookery.
Bob & Don out hauling trot lines — one red this am. abt .12 lbs.
Another flock of 2 doz or so willets — my flock joined them + took off down the shore line

Fri. aug. 16.
5:30 am.   very still - hot -
                  mosquitos - colum.
                  clouds piling up
                  overhead - bright
                  moon all night - no
                  fresh.
Night hawks — dozens of them over-
    head — "booming" as if it were
    mating time.
Heard night herons last night. People
    back in rookery before dawn.
    Some peep — spoiled any
    birding there.

Ruddy turnstones
rin. gulls
least terns — flocks of them, heading
    out toward bay.
People in rookery off + on all day.
man in jeep parked for an hour
or so — didn't see him leave
his car.

Looked for artesian well this p.m.

but failed to locate it — must be
dried up — found old concrete tank
but no signs of moisture.

5:30 pm.   Bob, Don + I hiked
across marshes to old shacks.
High heron rookery in clump of
cedar + chaparral by a running
salt water stream — back from
bay front. 3 dg or more adult
birds. Didn't go close enough
to see any young.

3 bl. neck stilts scolding mightily at
us.
1 Cormorant   overhead.
least terns, bl. terns
grackles, w. ibis
tri colored, spoonbills
am. egrets   all in abundance
                    through marshe.

This a.m. about 9 o'clock watched
Turkey vultures come over area.
        Least terns set up awful

Rockport - Big Tree   Aug. 21, 57
  Billy & John Jennings & Nancy
  Mildred & Brownie
  Cliff & Edie Fikes
  Bud, Don, Bob & I.

  Blue gray - gnatcatchers
  Poor wills & night heron -
    early mng. & dawn -
  shrike

  heron   Sept. 8
  Shrike -
  hummers fem.
                             Sept 10
  a. flycatchers
  male hummer
                             Sept 11
  bl-gr gnatcatch
  2 fem orioles   eating blackberries
                             Sept 18
Bl-ch. hummers (at wesutea (?))
  6 or 7 of them - some
  fly catching from telyph. wires
young poor will on li wire

Padre Isl. troop camp   Sept 21 + 2
                                 3, BC,
                              E.M?, S.C, N.Y
many willets +   Cathy, Bill Don
  turnstones on beach   John Jennings
    snowy plover
Weather bad -
  birds scarce
                                    23
Mockers, which have been
  absent about a month
  are back.
Cardinal young are feeding
  themselves. One young
  male caught by Smoky
  died next day. — not
 · using feeding station or
  window feeder now due
  to cat.
hummers still plentiful

first norther blew in last
  night — wet, but
  mild.

Oct 5
Mex Gr. Chat

Oct 9
1 am   (heard only)
4 am   birds migrating — high

Oct 24
No Water-thrush trapped in car —
After we released him he sat
on wire 5 feet O our heads &
eyed us saucily. Large, noisy
flock 1 geese about 7:30 pm.

Geese nearly every morning

62 Geese   7 a.m.   Nov. 3

visitors at feeding station
1.4.58 — myr. warbler
         dz song. sparrows
1.5.58 — ditto
         (warbler eating suet
          + seed)
1.6.58 - 7:30 am. mocker
1.8.58 - Cardinal (mal)
          myrtle warbler
1.11   - House wren

1-15 - 15 Cedar waxwings
        Cardinal 6 feeder E, da

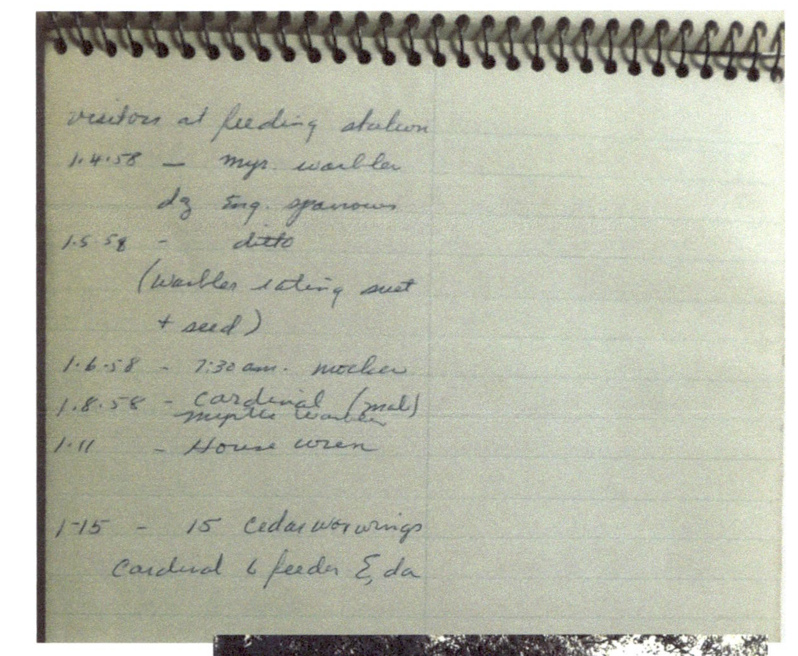

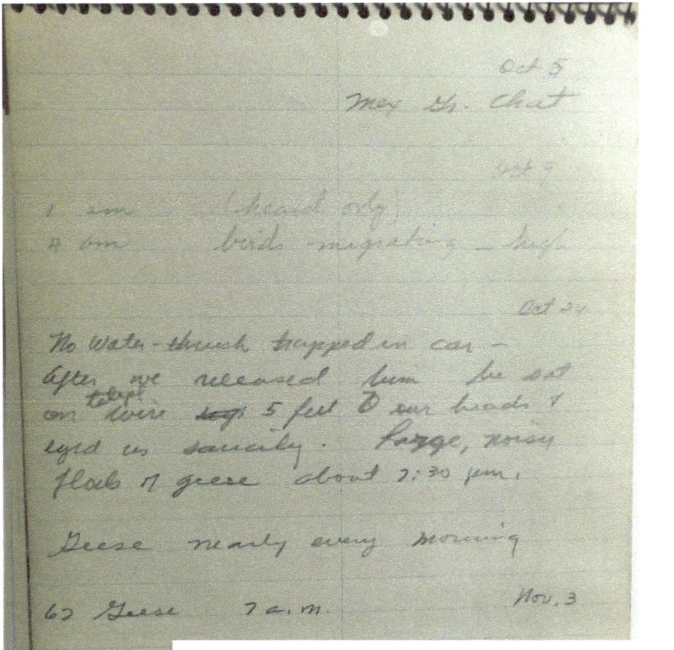

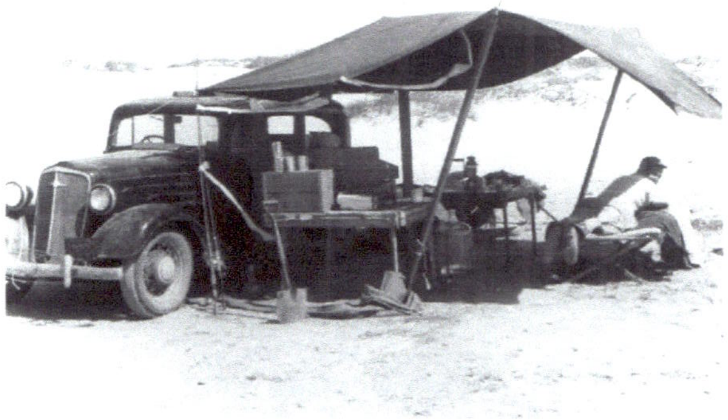

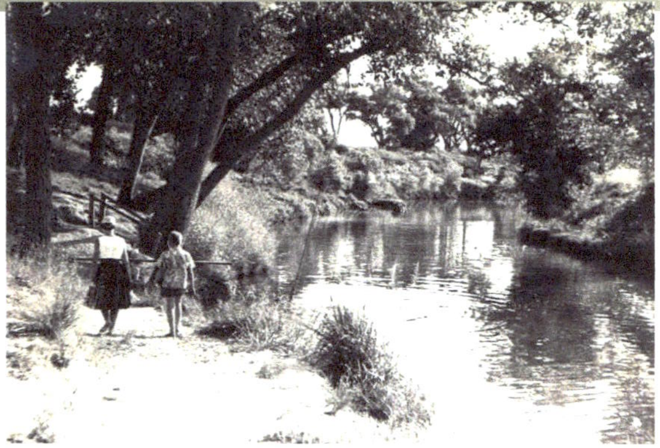

Mar. 9 /1958   abt 5 pm.   {Sr. Conf / Bus. Beds / Sally, Gail S
just South of Riviera
Swallow-tailed kite flew over
hiway. seen by entire party
12 turkey to left of hiway past RR tracks
((going down Mar. 7th abt 6 pm - dead
bobcat ~~to~~ at side of road. flat tire
abt 7 pm. - heard coyotes while
changing tire)) (Wildflowers in
bloom everywhere - huisache, yucca
verbena, wine cup, primrose, buttercup
vervain, phlox, asters, blue bonnets
many others uniden.)

Mar 12
Scissortail on telegh wire
in ~~S[illegible]~~ Belaire add.

3-16   md.
wh-eyed vireo
parula warb. ♂

yard
3/30   bl-gr gnatcatcher
yellow-bellied flycatcher

June 13 - Day Camp Site - Rushing
Blue Grosbeaks - male + young
came to feeding sta.

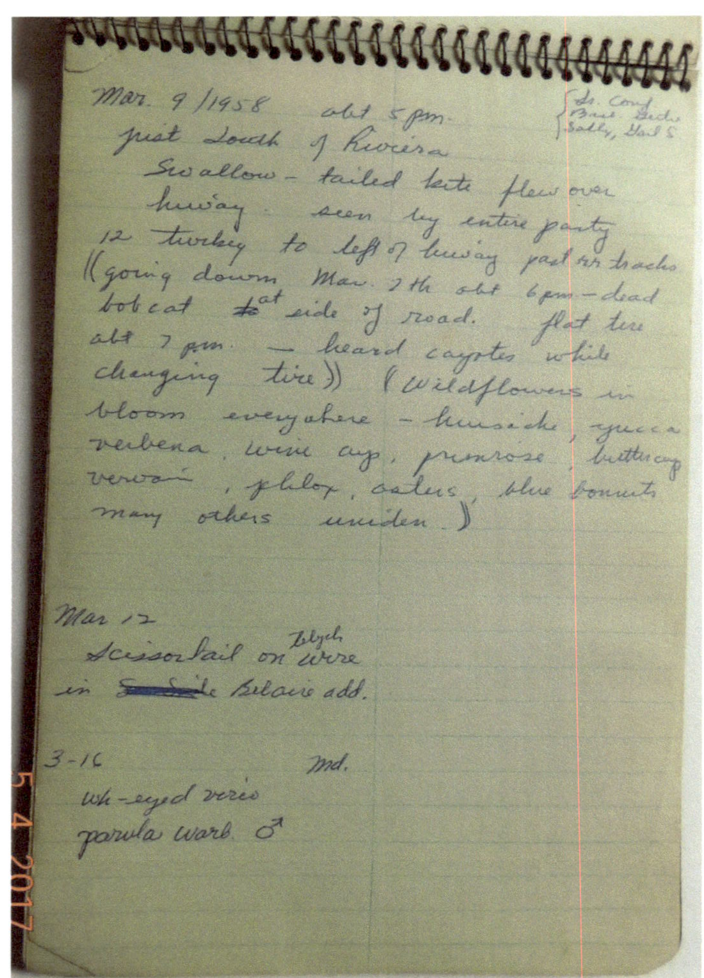

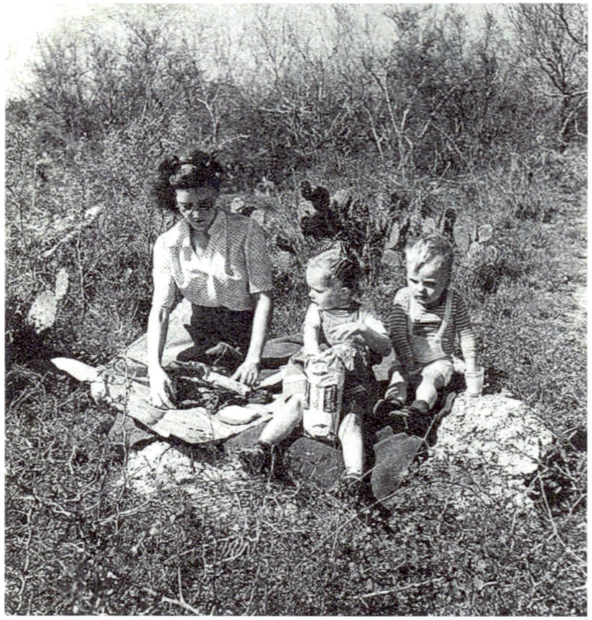

4-28-58   TO³ field out
Kent. Warb. ♂   last week
Painted bunt (song)   • Orchard oriole
                           Mourning w.

4-29-58   6:30 am
to hd cowbird ♂, ♀ at yard feeding sta.
heard cuckoo

5-8   4 pm.
yellow throat

5-9   fem red-eyed cowbird — eat bread crumbs

5-18   Canada warbler.
       redstart fem
       La Waterthrush
       Catbird
       nighthawks

939 432 01
807 841 41
Box 1958
N41, N4

comotion and flew at him, but
a ~~[crossed out]~~ black skimmer took
up the chase, flying above
+ diving on the vulture's back
until he took off in the
direction of Mission Bay.

Comet real good tonight (↑pm)
& last ni also

Sat. Aug. 17   Padre Is
              Home at 10:30 am.
              picked up Barbara
Browne & Mildred and came to
Padre.   Fish fry at 6 p.m.
Bob & Browne out in surf an
boat — very rough — no fish.

Sun. Aug 18
    up at 5 am.   Wind layed dn n
usual hr. pelicans (15 go So.) terns,
   bl. skimmers, turnstones, bl. terns
backs in dune heard chirps like warblers from
several directions — ~~turned~~ out to be ground
squirrels — must have mistaken this sound
for birds many times.   Home abt 6 p.m.

5/25
Mourning warb ♂

5/26
red-eyed vireos

6/6 Day Camp Site -Rushing property
Dickcissels sing ♀♀

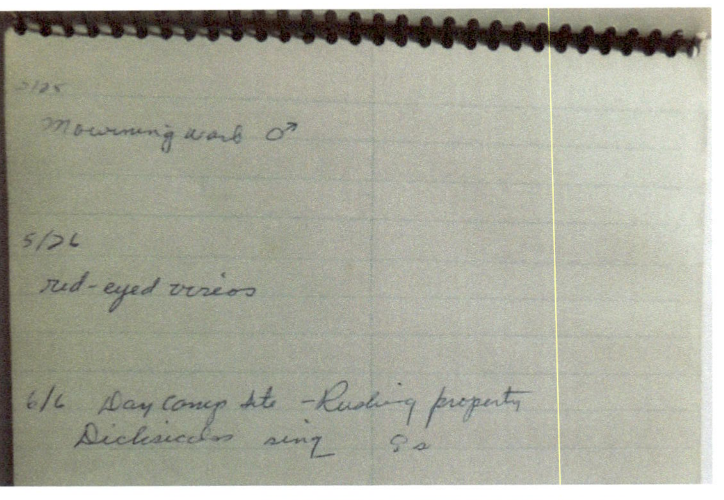

cometion and flew at him, but a ~~flock of~~ blacks skimmer took up the chase, flying above + diving on the vulture's back until he took off in the direction of Mission Bay.

Comet real good tonight (8pm) & last nt also

Sat. Aug. 17   Padre Is
Home at 10:30 am. picked up Barbara Browne & Mildred and came to Padre. Fish fry at 6 p.m. Bob & Browne out in surf an boat — very rough — no fish.

Sun. Aug 18
up at 5 am. Wind layed by n usual br. pelicans (15 go So.) terns, bl. skimmers, turnstones, bl. terns backs in dune heard chirps like warblers from several directions — turned out to be ground squirrels - must have mistaken this sound for birds many times. Home abt 6 p.m.

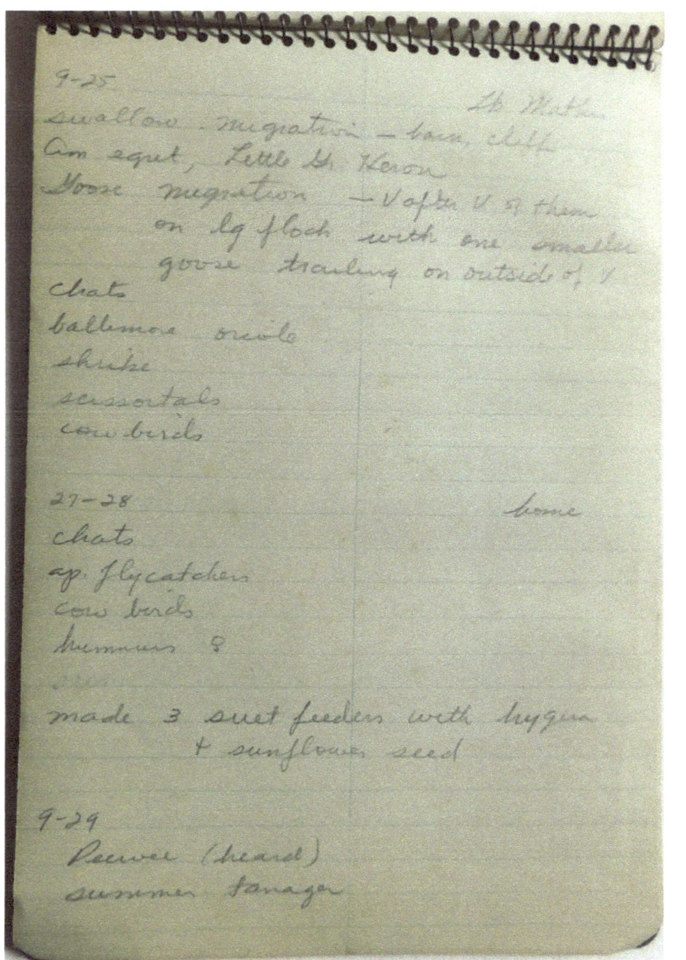

9-25   26 Mother
swallow migration — barn, cliff
Am egret, Little Gr. Heron
Goose migration — V after V of them
        on lg flock with one smaller
        goose trailing on outside of V
chats
baltimore oriole
shrike
scissortals
cow birds

27-28   home
chats
sp. flycatchers
cow birds
hummers 8

made 3 suet feeders with hygum
            + sunflower seed

9-29
Peewee (heard)
summer tanager

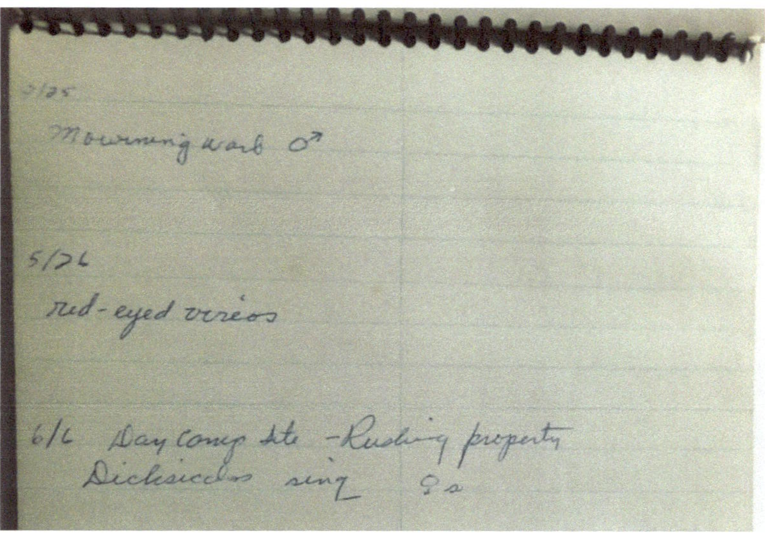

5/25
Mourning warb ♂

5/26
red-eyed vireos

6/6 Day comp site —Rusling property
     Dickisicdos sing   ♀♀

9-25
Lb. Mother
swallow migration — barn cliff
Am egret, Little G. Heron
Goose migration — V after V or them
    on lg flock with one smaller
    goose trailing on outside of V
chats
baltimore oriole
shrike
scissortals
cow birds

27-28   home
chats
sp. flycatchers
cow birds
hummus 8

made 3 suet feeders with hygen
    + sunflower seed

9-29
    Peewee (heard)
    summer tanager

10-13   Canada Warbler
    Geese — nearly every night

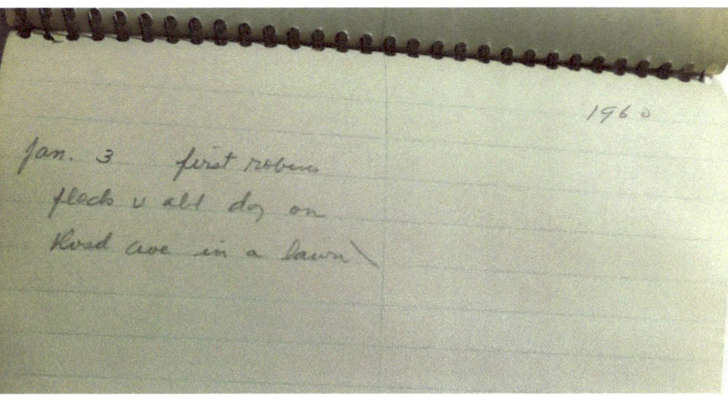

1960

Jan. 3   first robins
flock v all day on
Road ave in a lawn

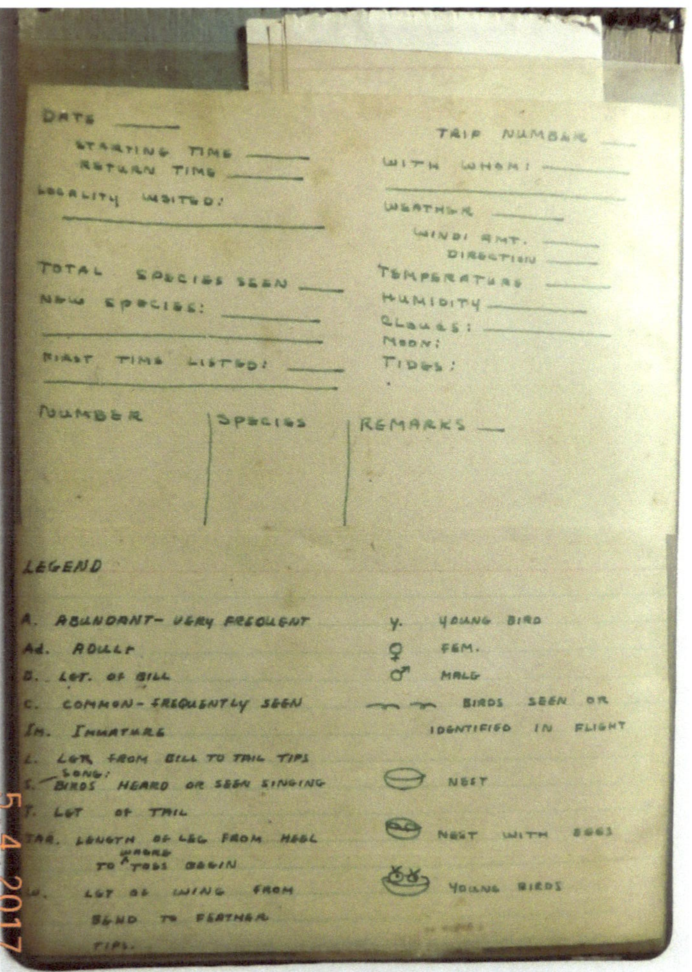

DATE ______
STARTING TIME ______
RETURN TIME ______
LOCALITY VISITED: ______

TRIP NUMBER ______
WITH WHOM: ______
WEATHER ______
WIND: AMT. ______
DIRECTION ______

TOTAL SPECIES SEEN ______
NEW SPECIES: ______
FIRST TIME LISTED: ______

TEMPERATURE ______
HUMIDITY ______
CLOUDS: ______
MOON: ______
TIDES: ______

NUMBER	SPECIES	REMARKS

LEGEND

A. ABUNDANT- VERY FREQUENT   Y. YOUNG BIRD
Ad. ADULT   ♀ FEM.
B. LGT. OF BILL   ♂ MALE
C. COMMON- FREQUENTLY SEEN   ~~ BIRDS SEEN OR
Im. IMMATURE   IDENTIFIED IN FLIGHT
L. LGT. FROM BILL TO TAIL TIPS
Song:
S. BIRDS HEARD OR SEEN SINGING   ⬭ NEST
T. LGT. OF TAIL
Tar. LENGTH OF LEG FROM HEEL   ⬭ NEST WITH EGGS
   WHERE TO TOES BEGIN
W. LGT. OF WING FROM   ⬭ YOUNG BIRDS
   BEND TO FEATHER
   TIPS.

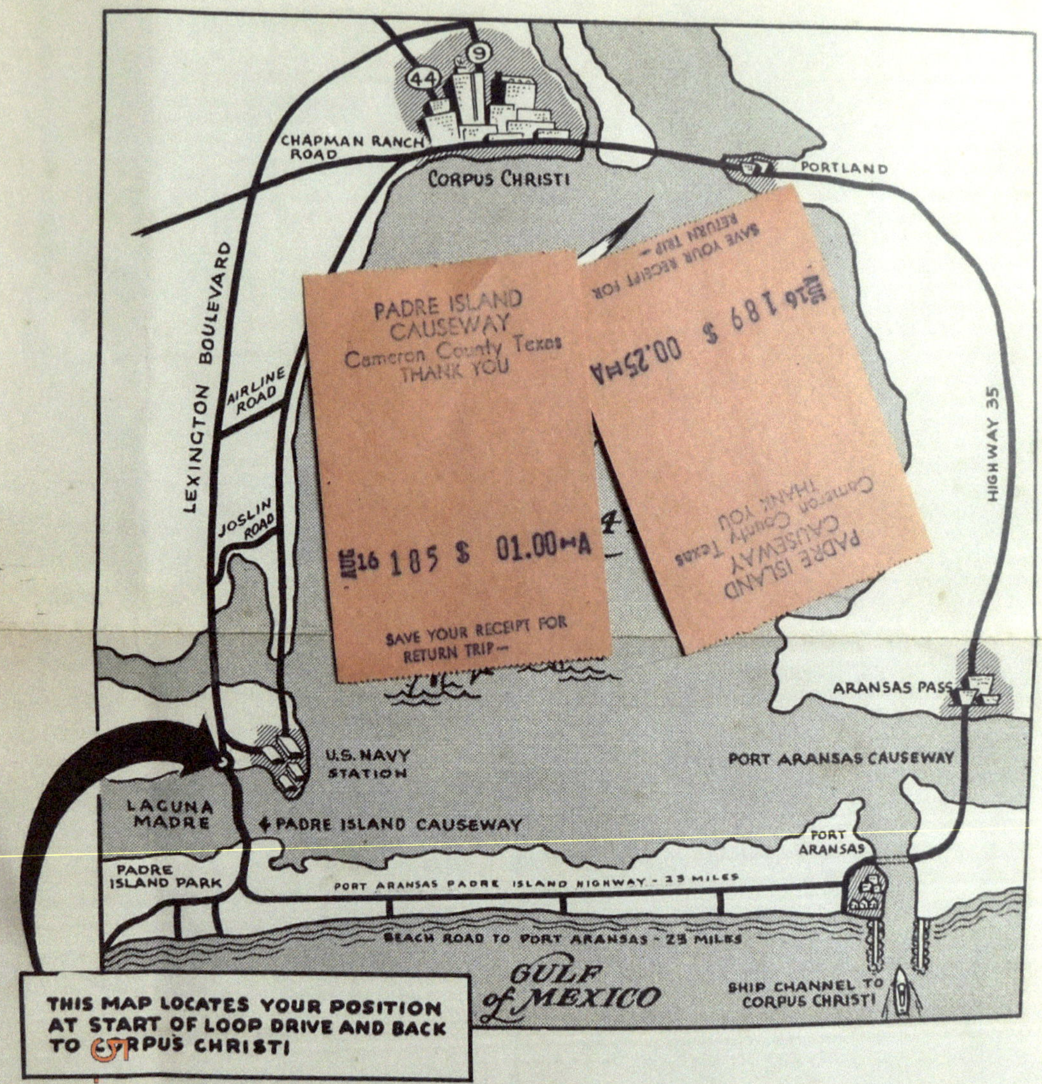

The causeway is operated without profit. Nueces County does not receive a penny from its operation, all profits being used to pay the cost of constructing the causeway. When the debt has been paid off the causeway will become a part of the State Highway system and will be maintained by the State Highway Commission free of tolls.

Thank you . . . Please save this round trip ticket. Present it at gate on return trip. You will be charged extra if you have no return ticket.

FOR YOUR INFORMATION

The Padre Island Causeway was opened to traffic on June 17, 1950. It cost $1,700,000. It is 3.9 miles long.

It crosses Laguna Madre, which separates most of the Coastal Bend Area of Texas from Padre Island. Laguna Madre covers 600 square miles. It extends from Corpus Christi to Port Isabel, a distance of 110 miles. There are several small islands in the lagoon. Two of these—Big and Little Bird Islands—are protected nesting grounds for many species of birds, including white pelicans.

The first bridge you come to after passing through the toll-gate is the Humble. This crosses the Humble Channel which permits the passage of ships to several oil wells.

FISHING FACILITIES

There are three baitstands at the Humble Bridge. Bait, tackle and boats are available. The baitstands are PARKER'S, FISHERMAN'S FOLLY and WRIGHT'S.

The second bridge is the Intracoastal. This crosses the famous Intracoastal Canal, which passes all the way down Laguna Madre and around the Gulf Coast to Florida.

Four baitstands and a cafe service fishermen at the Intracoastal Bridge. They are: GRAHAM'S, RED DOT, RUSH'S and OPAL'S CAFE.

A channel, 100 feet wide and 10 feet deep, extends along the causeway on the north side.

It is four miles across Padre Island, from the Causeway to the Gulf of Mexico. Enroute you will see the attractive Loma Alta Tourist Courts, and Benny's Drive In Restaurant.

At the Gulf Park, the 600-foot-long Bob Hall Pier provides a fine fishing facility. IRA's BAITSTAND is located at the foot of the Pier.

MUSEUM

The Padre Island Museum, a few hundred yards north of the Pier, is open from 1 to 5 p.m. weekdays, and from 11 a.m. to 5 p.m. Saturday, Sundays and Holidays.

A paved highway extends through the center of Padre and Mustang Islands, connecting the Padre Island and Port Aransas Causeways with access roads to the Gulf beach every 6 miles. This highway, finished recently, cost approximately $600,000.

Unless there is a high tide, you can drive the 51 miles along the beach between the two causeways.

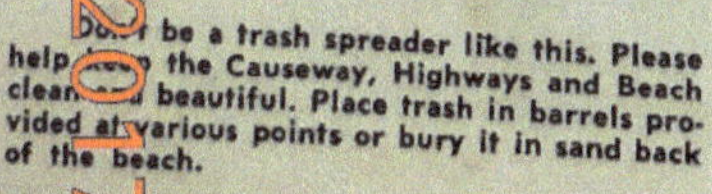

Don't be a trash spreader like this. Please help keep the Causeway, Highways and Beach clean and beautiful. Place trash in barrels provided at various points or bury it in sand back of the beach.

ONE LONG ISLAND

Padre and Mustang Islands formerly were separated by Corpus Christi Pass. The Pass is closed. So, the twin islands are in reality one, stretching along the Texas Coast 131 miles—from Port Aransas to Port Isabel.

Most of the year, you can drive down Padre Island for at least 28 miles. If in doubt, inquire at the toll-gate or at IRA'S BAITSTAND.

You are entering a fabulous, scenic land, rich in history and legends, populated by many species of birds, and rich with treasures from the sea.

Beginnings
The unfettered Spirit casting
about for a shore
drifts through eternity and the
unity of darkness.
It marks its path along the coast
of forever
and hovers like a gull devouring
the scraps of time.
photo & poem by
Barbara Kerr Scott

131

Dorothy Tilloson Kerr, born 17 July 1921 in Clegg, Texas, and died 6 July, 1993 in La Feria, Texas, devoted fifty-two of her seventy-two years to her dearest friend and husband, Robert Bruce Kerr (Bob). He devoted most of the last four years caring for her. Together they raised two children, dozens of domestic and feral animals, and hundreds of wild birds. OF all the creatures of this earth, apart from her family and close friends, she loved birds. Now, may her spirit soar with them.

Our name identifies us to ourselves and to other people. But, playing many roles in life, we have many more than the formal three words to which we have become accustomed. Known to most as Dorothy, she was born Baby Tilloson; her birth certificate still identifies her as Baby Tilloson.

As a child she was called Dorothy, and in school many addressed her by an affectionate modification of her last name, Tilly. Dad, that is, Bob, called her Dorothy, Honey, Your Mother (to me and Don) and occasionally, Mother, to which she invariably replied, "I'm not your mother." Don and I called her Mommy, Mother, and finally, Mom. My son, Robert Bruce, called her DoDo; this was actually an invention to echo the appellation he invented when he began naming things: he called Dad BoBo (boat-boat).

Mom's camp name was Sunny, and hundreds of Brownie Scouts, Girl Scouts, and counselors paid homage to that part of her personality which was happiest when camping. Of course, there were many who knew her as Mrs. Kerr. Finally, dozens of pet critters called her by the various onomatopoeia: Arf-Arf, Meow, Chirp, Tweet, and numerous varieties of squeak.

Mom was a very "private person," to use Dad's words. Actually, she was very shy, a rather strange thing to say about an adult; but, she kept things to herself, both likes and dislikes. Sometimes we can learn quite a bit about someone when we know what she liked and disliked.

Tops among her favorite books were various editions of the bible and the English dictionary; she probably had twenty volumes of each and a large copy of each ever open and ready on book stands.

I remember in particular *Kon Tiki*. When Don and I were quite young, probably close to the time of its publication, she read to all of us a chapter each evening on the front porch. I fondly remember the warm, breezy nights when there was plenty of time to talk about that voyage, and I could hardly wait for the next evening to hear another chapter. The adventure made such a strong impression that Mom and Dad named one of their boats Kon Tiki, and another one Kon Tiki II (and that one had an on-board 'convenience' which was called the Tiki).The Kon Tiki voyage and others that Thor Heyerdahl made were so important to the life of my imagination that I made a special effort to visit the Kon Tiki museum in Oslo one summer.

Another book, or in this case, author, was so important to Mom that he played a role in where Art and I elected to live for two years: Harry Golden. Mom was so taken with his

Only in America that she subscribed to *The Carolina Israelite* for years and read everything else that Mr. Golden wrote. When Bruce was about a year old Art got offers from two universities to teach sociology; he visited colleges in Dubuque and Charlotte, returning with good impressions of both. I lobbied hard to go to Charlotte because that is where Mr. Golden lived and I wanted to meet him. Not only did we move to Charlotte and meet him, where he inscribed copies of *Only in America* for Mom and for us with marvelous passages, but I also had the opportunity to finish my undergraduate work at Queens College.

Masters of the English language in one way or another were Mother's favorite authors. I learned the words to many Gilbert and Sullivan pieces at about the same time I was memorizing "The Night Before Christmas." To this day, I remember just as many words of "When I was a Lad" as I do of the Christmas poem.

Words, their origins and proper and clever uses, were a passion of hers. Thus, Shakespeare, Emily Dickinson, Will Cupy, Richard Armour, William Safire, Willard Espy, and other masters of *Our Marvelous Native Tongue* were her favorites. An early achievement of hers was so have served as editor of her high School newspaper for several years. Among other quotes, she copied these passages several times in her notes:

Her droll sense of humor played delightfully on the eccentricities and potentialities of the English language. Modifying the inane utterances we hear every day was one of her specialities – things you wouldn't likely notice unless you were listening closely: "half of one and six dozen of the other," or, in rare form when I left for a date once, "remember, familiarity breeds." At one point during her final weeks Dad asked (about me), "Do you think she gets her smarts form me?" to which she replied, "'Must have: I still have mine." (Don't worry, folks, he still has enough smarts for two people.)

In one of her latest notes, obviously part of a recent conversation with someone, she wrote, "I've asked Barbara if she ever missed Trick-or-Treating on Halloween and she said, 'No'. I've never asked Don: I really don't like Halloween." This attitude is characteristic of her strong sense of moral right, making her an ideal mentor and model for her children, her friends, and the dozens of Girl Scouts who were members of her Girl Scout Troop #30 for ten years.

These moral convictions and actions, I think, made her admire John Kennedy, who began to equal Truman in her esteem in the early 1960s. She often referred to the movie, *To Kill a Mockingbird*, which touched on those issues so important to her. Her opposition to every form of prejudice and segregation inspired me to speak out in my last year of high school in Florida to the extent that I had only one friend that year.

Not only did she firmly believe in fairness, and counsel a sharp distinction between right and wrong, she believed in playing by the rules. For instance, she really hated seat belts and refused to wear them -- until it became the law. After that, she always wore them, grudgingly, but she wore them. I think it would be hard to find a more honest person, with herself, and with others.

I greatly value her commitment to critical thought which grew out of her concepts of right and wrong and fairness. Through Mom's and Dad's examples, discussions, and her taste in reading, I was nurtured on evaluating ideas and information. I am grateful for having been given these skills as a child, for I can see through my teaching experiences that they are extremely difficult to cultivate in an adult.

A few things Mom simply couldn't tolerate: most significant among these were unfairness, prejudicial behavior, segregation, dishonesty, gossip, vulgar language, and a trivial irritation with which I also identify – those small pieces of cardboard stapled inside your magazines.

Mom loved animals and spent innumerable hours bird watching. She kept detailed notes of her sightings for over four decades. I was so impressed at an early age with the importance of birds to our environment that I still take note when a count is taken of the Whooping Cranes.

We also collected a wonderful variety of pets, from the normal varieties of dogs and an occasional cat, to several kinds of squirrels and two skunks (a striped variety we called Stinky, and a spotted one we called Smelody), to several species of rescued wild birds. Cheeper, an English Sparrow, lived with us a long time, and would eat from one's mouth. Sandy was a Boat-Tailed Grackle who lived in the yard at least two years. We could never get a single word out of our two parakeets, Pete and RePete. Teki, short for Tequilla, a descendant of two other pet Chihuahuas, Mitzi and Toddy, could fit in Dad's shirt pocket. Mom's last pets, a menagerie of five Road Runners, a large dog, and a couple of adopted strays who provided hours of entertainment as they grew from clown-kittens into cats, all seemed to be oblivious to one another as they promoted their special needs on the front porch.

Camping provided some of my most cherished memories and helped shape how I live and cope today. Naming it for a popular song of the early fifties, "What's Behind the Green Door," she painted the doors of our home-made camping rig green and printed *Green Door* above them. We still talk about the *Green Door* and our unique adventures hauling it behind one vehicle or another, usually the white jeep with a black canvas top, isinglass windows, red wheels, and a brass donkey hood ornament. Through scouting, which was another avenue to camping I learned another valuable lesson from Mother: she impressed upon me that if I wanted my special dream to come true, to become an International Scout, I would have to be the first to speak up at meetings to be perceived as a leader. That was a tough nut to crack, but I still remember and apply that rule today, for two years after I began to follow that advice I was selected as an International Scout. I simply could not have done it without her.

Unfortunately, many of us often think of her as a victim of cancer; however, she didn't see herself this way. Her sense of self respect and dignity were never marred by the dreadful disease, which, over four years modified her body. If anything, it seemed to strengthen her character and solidify her determination to get the highest quality from each day. She lived a full and fruitful threescore and ten, and more.

Letter from Dorothy Kerr to "Skipper" mid August 1970   (Celia hit CC late Aug 3, 1970)

Dear Skipper,
      Here's why I'm so late in responding ti your nice phone call. "Celia" aimed a cruel blow at us that afternoon. You can take just about anything you heard about it - add a little to it - and be near the truth. As you know, I've lived in hurricane country all my life - in Corpus Christi and elsewhere. I don't even get really excited when one is coming. "Celia" was much worse than anything before; there just isn't any comparison.
      I left the office shortly after you called. She was supposed to have diminished to 90 m.p.h. at that time. By the time I got home - 30 minutes or so - the report had been changed. She was packing winds of over 130 mph & headed straight for us. The eye hit downtown CC at over 160 mph - the weather equipment was lost at that point - and practically demolished downtown Corpus Christi o the main drag, I mean.
      We live 21 miles away. It removed our 2-car carport completely and a cabaña we had on the waterfront. It destroyed half of our enclosed garage, the garage roof, and a big chunk of the house roof.
      Yes, we were in the house.
      I was standing in the kitchen and could have reached out the window and touched the carport when it went sailing off. I'll never forget that sound. It's impossible to describe the sound of a building being ripped from its foundation all at once in a matter of 2 or 3 minutes.
      By this time there was so much junk flying around we couldn't leave. I don't think I was born with enough sense to be scared, but I was somewhat worried!
      Our store buildings (Gunderland's) are less than 2 years old, house the leading ship chandelling business in Corpus Christi as well, and industrial supplies and the pleasure boat trade. We have quite a large layout. We lost the built-up roof and part of a concrete brick wall. We're still taking inventory of wind and water damaged merchandise.
      We also have a second store (Gunderland's Boatland) where we sell and service Chris-Craft and other large boats). The entire building was damaged. Kenneth Gunderland lost his entire home. Four other employees had roof and structural damage. With the exception of 2 or 3, all our 31 employees had minor damage.
      Bob & I have had a camp-travel trailer - practically brand new. It rolled over a couple of times and is a total wreck. We have an old Thunderbird cruiser ('66) and a brand new Glastron run-about (delivered 3 weeks before Celia). Both were damaged , the new one seriously (as well as practically every other boat stored here at Gunderland's).
      But somebody up there likes us, though we surely don't deserve it. Few were injured. Only 4 deaths can be blamed directly on "Celia," though several heart attacks were, no doubt, indirectly caused.. Only 7 deaths in Corpus Christi. When you look at block after block & mile of wrecked homes and businesses it is hard to imagine why hundreds were not killed.
      We have managed to move the roof & wall sections out of our yard - Bob dragged them out with the truck. (We own the lot next door, so we didn't have far to drag them.) We cut our beautiful trees back to good wood, merely skeletons of their former size, and

have our yard in pretty good shape. We are unable to get a contractor, and, from all indications, it may be 3 or 4 months before we do. So, along with the hundreds of other families in Corpus Christi, the Kerrs are camping at home for the duration. Both of our cars were in the carport and neither was touched. This is one of those odd things that happens in a hurricane. By all rights they should have been crushed flat.

And the clean up goes on.

Now, where were we before the storm?….[irrelevant text omitted here]. I was a little distracted when we talked August 3rd. – I'll never forget that date! I even lost the notepad I wrote your address on and had to call the Chamber of Commerce to look it up in their Jacksonville directory. Fact is, my office was such a mess I couldn't find anything except what was in the safe and vault. I still have the habit of putting my work away every day. No important records were lost, though some were wet.

I didn't intend to write you a book - just thought you might enjoy an eye witness account.

Now tell me about {irrelevant text omitted].… reminds me of the sad fate of the little Barracuda run-about we brought back from Jacksonville. We sold it to some long-time friends for their son, who was the same age and a friend of Gene McDonald's. Two weeks later he and a friend took it to a lake at Austin to ski. They wrecked the boat and both boys drowned. It makes you wonder sometimes - is pleasure boating really worth it!

[irrelevant text omitted]….Your friend, Dorothy Kerr

Roof & carport on their way into the canal

Severe damage to a bird watching venue, courtesy of Hurricane Celia (Nassau Drive, Corpus Christi)

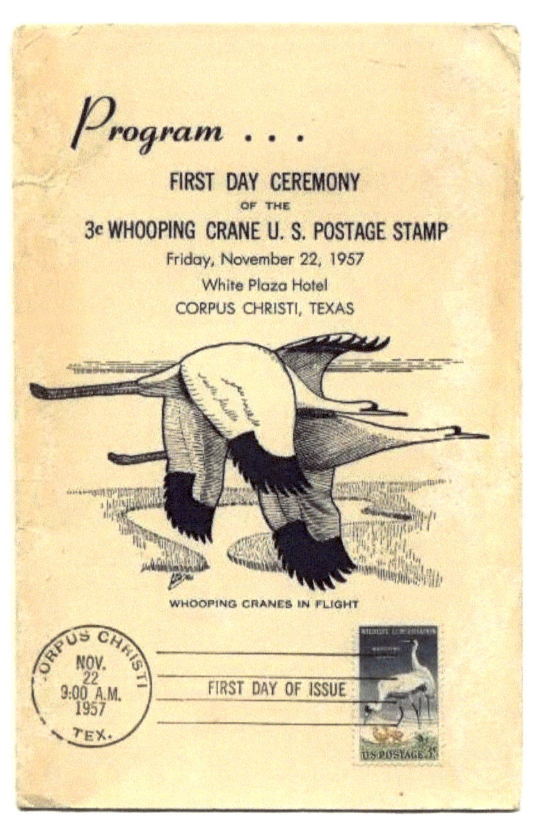

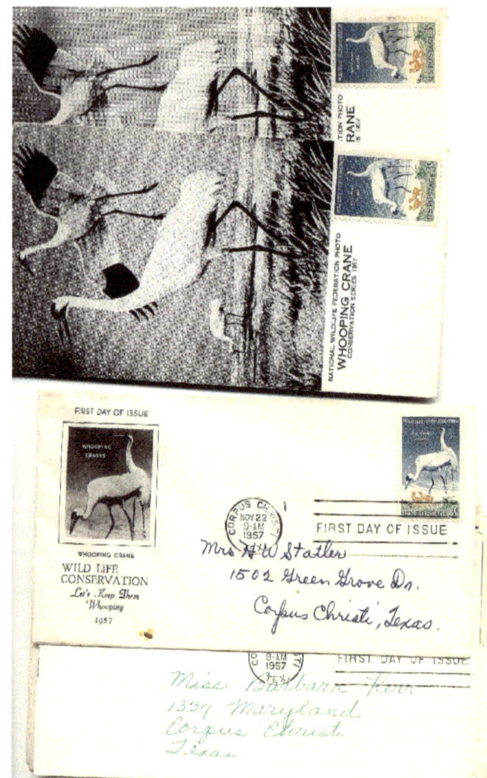

The Whooping Crane

Once a fairly abundant species, the whooping crane has become one of America's three rarest birds. The only flock left in the wild numbers from 25 to 39 and makes its winter home on Blackjack Peninsula on the Texas Coast, now a part of the 47,000 acre Aransas National Wildlife Refuge about 65 miles from Corpus Christi. In the spring they migrate to the vicinity of Wood Buffalo National Park in Canada's Northwest Territories. In October and November they return to Aransas Refuge, a flight of 1,300 miles.

Formerly whooping cranes ranged through mid-continental America, summering from Utah as far east as South Carolina and as far south as Mexico. Their summer nesting grounds extended into the United States bordering Canada.

Two major factors have threatened the whoopers with extinction: One may be attributed to their own ways, the other to the ways of man.

The whooping crane demands a certain kind of feeding range, it must have both fresh and salt water and the marshy growth that accompany these waters. They eat acorns and other plant life as well as crayfish and other small marine life. A pair of adult birds requires a range of at least a square mile of such terrain to support it. As the continent became settled and land was cleared for agriculture, the suitable territory for the whooper shrunk. The land could no longer support large numbers.

Man further became a hazard with his gun. Hunters, intrigued by the size of the great bird, brought him down for trophies. After it was put on the protected list and a penalty assessed for shooting the whooping crane, hunters claimed they mistook them for snow geese, ibis or white pelicans. Such a mistake is unforgivable and unnecessary.

(Continued on Back Page)

PROGRAM

4:00 P. M., November 22, 1957

Presiding — Mr. Jack Blackmon

INVOCATION — Mr. J. Frank LaRoe

GREETINGS — Mr. John Nugent, Corpus Christi Chamber of Commerce

INTRODUCTION AND REMARKS —

The Honorable John Young, Congressman
The Honorable Robert Hemphill, Congressman
The Honorable Ralph Scott, Congressman

PRESENTATION OF FIRST DAY SETS —

Miss Alice Lee Erickson, President, Sea Gull Stamp Club

REMARKS by The Honorable Ormonde A. Kieb, in charge of Bureau of Facilities, Post Office Department, and Presentation of Autographed Albums.

* * *

6:00 P. M. — Banquet.

Speaker: Dr. Clarence Cottam, Director, Rob & Bessie Welder Wildlife Foundation.

Thousands Of Crane Stamps Sold

It was Whooping Crane Day in Corpus Christi yesterday, with thousands of commemorative wildlife conservation stamps and first-day covers sold.

The whooping crane, the subject of the fourth conservation stamp, was fittingly honored by members of the Sea Gull Stamp Club, conservation enthusiasts, and the Corpus Christi Chamber of Commerce.

The day began at 7 a.m. when windows opened at the Corpus Christi post office for sale of the Whooping Crane Stamp.

Movie Caps Day

The day was concluded with the showing of a movie at the White Plaza Hotel following a dinner attended by philatelists and wild life conservation groups.

The Whooping Crane was emphasized throughout the day as a fitting symbol of America's interest in conserving the nation's wild life.

Rep. John Young, a member of the House Civil Service and Postal Affairs Committee, and two colleagues from the committee, Rep. Ralph Scott (D-NC) and Rep. Robert W. Hemphill (D-SC), attended the dinner last night and ceremonies conducted by the stamp club and the Corpus Christi Chamber of Commerce in the afternoon.

The ceremonies were part of a three-day philatelic exhibit on the Deck at the White Plaza Hotel.

Stamp Dealers on Hand

The exhibit was attended by a number of stamp dealers, and first-day covers and Whooping Crane Stamps were available during the day.

A movie on wild life in South Texas will be shown at the exhibit at 11 a.m. today, Miss Alice Lee Erickson, president of the stamp club, said.

Whooper 'Majestic' Bird

Dr. Clarence Cottam, director of the Rob and Bessie Welder Wildlife Refuge at Sinton, described the whooping crane as the most majestic of marsh and coastline birds.

Speaking at the dinner, Cottam said the whooping cranes at the Aransas Wildlife Refuge are worth "more than a million dollars" to Texas as a tourist attraction.

But more valuable, Cottam said, is the value of the birds as symbols of America's determination to preserve its natural resources through intelligent conservation.

Dignitaries To Attend Stamp Day

Wildlife Director Will Be Principal Speaker at Dinner

Three congressmen and the assistant postmaster general will participate in Friday afternoon ceremonies scheduled by the Sea Gull Stamp Club for the first-day-of-issue of the Whooping Crane Stamp.

The 4 p.m. ceremonies on the Deck of the White Plaza Hotel will be presided over by Jack Blackmon. Congressman John Young (D-Texas), Robert Hemphill (D. N. C.) and Ralph Scott (D-S. C.) will be introduced for brief talks.

Ormonde A. Kieb, assistant postmaster general in charge of facilities, Washington, D.C., will present autograph albums to city, state, wildlife and stamp people.

Dr. Clarence Cottam, director of the Rob and Bessie Welder Wildlife Foundation, will be principal speaker at a 6 p.m. dinner that evening on the Deck of the White Plaza Hotel. Members of the Corpus Christi Outdoor Club will be special guests at the two afternoon ceremonies.

A three-day philatelic exhibit on the White Plaza Deck will be opened in conjunction with the first day ceremonies. Alice Lee Erickson, Sea Gull Stamp Club president, said. The exhibit will be of 75 frames consisting of many fine frames including two gold medal winning collections from out of state.

Awards are to be presented in three classifications to exhibits judged best in the show. Jack Deforrest, Jr., is chairman of the show which will be climaxed with an auction at 7:30 p.m. Sunday.

Photographs: Bird Watching Venues
in order of appearance

Dorothy Tilloson	Del Mar College classroom, 1941
Dorothy, Barbara & Don	Nueces River Park
	Nueces River path
Home, Green Grove Drive	Where many observations were made, 1951
Dorothy	Lake Mathis or Inks Lake
Camp Rig	Padre Island, early 50's
Barbara & Don	Devil's River, 1954
Barbara & Don	Goose Island, about 1944
Barbara & Don	Big Oak, Rockport, 1950
Dorothy, Barbara & Don	Pecos River area, 1954
Dorothy	Dailey's Camera Store, 1941
Dorothy	Dailey's Camera Store, 1941
Beginnings & Photo	Barbara Kerr Scott (Tribute to Mom)
Hurricane Celia Damage	Nassau St., Corpus Christi, August, 1970
Program & Cachets	collection
Corpus Christi Times articles	by permission

This page

Picnic site	Sinton park, 1950
Padre Island	1962. 1947
Guadalupe River	1953